MAKING RESEARCH MATTER
Steps to Impact for Health and Care Researchers

Tara Lamont

First published in Great Britain in 2021 by

Policy Press, an imprint of
Bristol University Press
University of Bristol
1–9 Old Park Hill
Bristol
BS2 8BB
UK
t: +44 (0)117 954 5940
e: bup-info@bristol.ac.uk

Details of international sales and distribution partners are available at
policy.bristoluniversitypress.co.uk

British Library Cataloguing in Publication Data
A catalogue record for this book is available from the British Library

ISBN 978-1-4473-6115-2 paperback
ISBN 978-1-4473-6116-9 OA ePub
ISBN 978-1-4473-6117-6 OA ePdf

Cover design by Liam Roberts
Front cover image: Floortja/Nndanko/Bgblue/Liam Roberts
Bristol University Press and Policy Press use environmentally responsible
print partners.
Printed and bound in Great Britain by CMP, Poole

It is curious that people should think a report self-executive, should not see that, when the report is finished, the work begins.

Florence Nightingale, letter to
Mary Elizabeth Herbert (1863)

Evidence does not speak for itself, but needs to be mobilised at the right time, and through the right people, to make a difference in decision-making.

Swan et al, Evidence in
Management Decisions, *2012*

Contents

List of figures and boxes   vi
List of interviews   viii
Acknowledgements   ix

1	Introducing this book	1
2	WHY researchers should spend time on this	11
3	WHAT counts as evidence	25
4	WHO you want to reach – practitioners	41
5	WHO you want to reach – patients, public, service users	63
6	WHO you want to reach – policymakers and managers	84
7	WHEN you could have most impact	104
8	HOW to reach people – use of stories and the media	114
9	HOW to reach people – finding the right language and style	138
10	Last thoughts	159

Notes   167
Further reading   169
References   174
Index   195

List of figures and boxes

Figures

1.1	Cartoon – then a miracle occurs	3
3.1	Stakeholders rating research on specialist palliative care	39
4.1	Working with partner organisations	56
5.1	Testing displays of data for parents of children undergoing heart surgery	66
5.2	Comic book bringing to life research on weight and stigma	70
5.3	Service users making sense of research	74
5.4	Patient experiences vignettes to illustrate research	78
5.5	Easy-read version of research on learning disability services	80
6.1	Prioritising engagement activity according to the evidence – what works in research use	97
8.1	Twitter as a source of creativity	129
8.2	Use of infographics	136

Boxes

2.1	Five steps for better engagement	21
3.1	Research example – social prescribing	26
3.2	Research example – protective clothing	30
3.3	Interview – Ghazala Mir	32
3.4	Involving end users in finding research which matters	38
4.1	Research examples – research which changes practice	42
4.2	Interview – Eileen Shepherd	44
4.3	Interview – Elaine Maxwell	47
4.4	Using practitioner quotes and insights	52
4.5	Interview – Sui Ting Kong	53

4.6	Interview – Godfred Boahen	55
4.7	Interview – Teresa Chinn	58
4.8	Interview – Jack Chew	60
5.1	Research example – use of emergency services	64
5.2	Research example – how parents understand risk	67
5.3	Research example – understanding obesity	68
5.4	Interview – Sally Crowe	71
5.5	Interview – Peter Beresford	75
6.1	Research example – talking therapies	85
6.2	Research example – safer staffing	87
6.3	Interview – Peter Griffiths	88
6.4	Interview – Paul Cairney	89
6.5	Interview – Nancy Hey	94
6.6	Briefings for politicians	99
6.7	Tips for researchers to influence policy	101
7.1	Research example – stroke configuration	107
7.2	Research example – home oximetry monitoring	108
7.3	Interview – Naomi Fulop	109
7.4	Research example – sharing emerging evidence on Long COVID	110
8.1	Interview – Shaun Lintern	115
8.2	Research example – air quality	122
8.3	Interview – Clint Witchalls	125
8.4	Research example – understanding inpatients with dementia	132
9.1	Plain language summaries – two examples	142
9.2	Writing for impact – key features	146
9.3	Titles which pull readers in	147
9.4	Summary headlines – from academic to journalistic	150
9.5	Research example – green spaces	151

List of interviews

Ghazala Mir, researcher on health and social inequalities
Eileen Shepherd, clinical editor, *Nursing Times*
Elaine Maxwell, nurse and research engagement lead
Teresa Chinn, nurse and social media specialist, founder @WeNurses
Jack Chew, physiotherapist and founder, *Physio Matters* podcast
Godfred Boahen, social work practice and research lead
Sui Ting Kong, researcher on social work and practitioner research lead
Sally Crowe, patient and public involvement lead in healthcare and research
Peter Beresford, service user and researcher in mental health and disability
Peter Griffiths, researcher on healthcare workforce
Paul Cairney, researcher on politics and public policy
Nancy Hey, director of the What Works Wellbeing Centre
Naomi Fulop, researcher in healthcare organisation and management
Shaun Lintern, health correspondent, *The Independent*
Clint Witchalls, health and medicine editor, *The Conversation*

Acknowledgements

This book is dedicated to Linda Lamont, for her long support for health services and the stories that lie behind.

My thanks to the named interviewees and research contributors in this book whose insights and commitment to getting evidence used shine through.

I am also grateful to Philippa Grand and colleagues at Policy Press for steering this work so skilfully and to the anonymous reviewers who strengthened this book from early drafts.

My thanks to Kate Searle for help with images and general communications know-how.

For stimulus and support on all matters research and engagement over the years, my particular thanks to:

Elaine Maxwell (and then some), Matt Westmore, Andree Le May, John Gabbay, Steph Garfield-Birkbeck, Ruairidh Milne, Frances Healey, Beverley Fitzsimons, Liz Mear, Annette Boaz, Helen Mthiyane, Kieran Walshe, Judith Smith, Naomi Fulop, Jo Rycroft-Malone, Robbie Foy, Huw Davies, Martin Roland, Jane Ball, Carl Macrae, Sarah Scobie, Richard Thomson, Tansy Evans, Peter Davidson, Alison Ford, Rob Squire, Rob Cook, Eugenia Cronin, Dez Holmes, Louise Wallace, Sally Redman and Elaine Williams.

1

Introducing this book

Getting your research into the world

Florence Nightingale was prescient in noting the effort needed to promote and engage people in research. Evidence rarely speaks for itself or, in her words, is 'self-executive' (McDonald 2005). In her own work around the report to the Indian Sanitary Commission, she worked tirelessly and skilfully – 'four heavy years' – to create demand for the finished product. This included lobbying MPs and working with policymakers at all levels to improve health and hygiene of ordinary soldiers. The final report was a magisterial two-volume affair of over 2,000 pages, with data and statistics from a survey of all military stations in India.

Her genius was to add 23 pages of her own 'observations', essentially her commentary on the data, including free-text summaries and stories from the thousands of pages of survey returns. These were attractive, accessible and illustrated with woodcuts. Grouped under readable headings, from overcrowding to diet, they included her own acerbic analysis, pulling no punches – 'There is no drainage, in any sense in which we understand the word. The reports speak of cesspits as if they were dressing-rooms' (Cook 1913). These popular texts had mass circulation and were sent and promoted to public people of standing from John Stuart Mill to (even) Queen Victoria. Abridged versions of the whole report were distributed in advance to military and medical officers, with commendations and forewords from people of influence. She briefed journalists and sent early review copies to appear in periodicals, from *The Economist* to *The Spectator*. In effect, she created 'pull' for the report with recommendations for reform which was published in 1863.[1]

We may not all have the ear of royalty. But there are some general lessons for us all on how best to create impact for research. This includes tailoring outputs for your audience, spending time on summaries and short versions, bringing issues to life with stories and case studies, identifying people of influence for those you want to reach who can act as champion and interpreter of your work. It means being active in mobilising your research.

But researchers may not realise what steps are needed to get their research used. The 1977 cartoon by Sydney Harris in Figure 1.1 illustrates beautifully the magical thinking of many that research on its own will effortlessly influence practice or thinking.

If researchers think at all about how their findings could be made more useful or accessible, they tend to fix on certain kinds of output. As director of a national evidence centre, I was often approached by universities or researchers to share my knowledge about reaching non-academic audiences. Some teams would ask if they should develop an animation or toolkit at the end of the project. My advice was always to focus first on the people they were trying to reach, their channels and interests, before the products.

What is the point of this book?

Much has been written about research impact and the evidence-practice gap, but largely to and for academic audiences. This book will give researchers a deeper understanding of some of these debates and challenges, while offering some practical solutions to strengthening and framing research for different audiences. Different outputs and approaches may be needed for different evidence users, whether they are carers of people with dementia, directors of adult social care services or lead pharmacists. This

Figure 1.1: Cartoon – then a miracle occurs

Source: Copyrighted artwork by Sydney Harris Inc. All materials used with permission.

book aims to extract the best of current thinking on increasing research uptake, with practical tips and insights from leading journalists, practitioners, editors and other experts who know how to get people's attention in the right way.

I draw on five years' experience leading work at a national centre to disseminate research to the health service, as well as several years as one of the editors for a journals series and as an adviser to a national research programme assessing health service projects for relevance and rigour. But my interest in how people read and write stories goes way back. Before a career in health policy and research management, with some further training in statistics and social policy, I did an English degree and enjoyed the chance to study how texts work and the ways in which different groups of readers at different times make sense of these narratives. One of my messages throughout this book is to bring your whole self to your research project, taking inspiration from thinkers and writers who appeal to you, not just in your chosen field.

Who is this book for?

This book is designed for researchers in health and social care wanting to make a difference. It combines an overview of some of the main threads of recent scholarly debate, with worked examples of research which has made impact in interesting ways and pointers for further reading. It may stimulate some readers to dig deeper into emerging academic fields. But others may just want to get a broad understanding and focus on some of the practical lessons for making their research outputs more relevant and compelling.

Information in this book may be particularly useful for those at early stages of their career, including doctoral and postdoctoral researchers, junior lecturers and independent researchers. But more senior researchers, experienced in submitting papers to academic journals, may benefit too from advice on the different approaches needed to reach wider audiences. It may also be helpful for those with responsibility for training and developing early career researchers, as well as funding bodies and research managers wanting to maximise the uptake and impact of research which they fund or support.

My focus is on health and care, paying particular attention to researchers working in healthcare management, nursing, allied health and social care practice and policy. These fields have been underserved in the past, with debates on evidence-based care often focusing on medicine. There is a growing number of non-medical practitioners engaged in research, and many of the most pressing uncertainties of the day need high-quality contributions from these fields. This book will provide worked examples and practical tips drawing on research relevant to managers, nurses, allied health professionals and social care practitioners.

A key message in this book is that effective engagement and influence takes time and skill. For researchers working in a particular field, it can mean developing and sustaining long-term relationships with the right individuals or partner organisations over many years and working with them to communicate research findings. It is not realistic to expect everyone on the team to do this (or want to do this). But they may need to understand why this is important to do. As noted by Davies and colleagues:

> It may be most fruitful in academia to promote a common acknowledgement of the importance and value of sharing and applying appropriate bodies of research in policy and practice settings, but not to expect that all researchers will have the skills or desire to actively engage in knowledge mobilisation activities. (Davies et al 2015: 130)

This book should provide a foundation for all researchers interested in getting their research used. Not everyone needs to be an expert knowledge broker or influencer themselves. Some of the examples I mention may inspire you to get in touch with your university communications team to think about a social media campaign or event with a partner organisation. You may want to try writing a blog or feature article with a dementia advocacy group. Understanding the expertise of others, whether those with lived experience or knowledge of strategic communications, is an important part of getting your research more widely used.

How is this book structured?

This book follows four main dimensions of the journey of evidence into practice. It covers the WHAT, WHO, WHEN and HOW of research in seven short chapters, drawing on a helpful parallel framework for impact literacy (Bayley and Phipps 2019). Before this, Chapter 2 sets out WHY researchers should spend time thinking about the way their findings will be used and provides an overarching strategic framework for engagement. Chapter 3 then looks at the WHAT of evidence itself, the kinds of knowledge which 'count' as legitimate evidence and will be relevant to decision-makers. This includes a discussion on quality of evidence and how researchers can make their work stand out without adding to information overload for busy readers.

The most important aspect for researchers is to consider WHO their research is for. Chapters 4–6 look at audiences who might use research, starting with practitioners and a particular focus on nursing, allied health and social care communities. This draws on debates about how research outputs can be contextualised for practice settings, recognising professional wisdom and insights. Chapter 5 considers the needs of the general public, patients or service users, for accessible forms of research findings which are not over-simplified. This is followed by Chapter 6, drawing on knowledge of how policymakers make decisions and use research in the real world. These three chapters are structured by the five steps for successful engagement strategy set out at the end of Chapter 2. Worked examples are used to illustrate how researchers have engaged with stakeholders and developed tailored outputs for and with different audiences. These chapters include tips from valued informants on how to maximise relevance and appeal. This is followed by an account in Chapter 7 of WHEN research can have most impact, considering policy and practice 'windows' which can be exploited.

Having considered audiences and timing, two chapters look in more detail at HOW research is presented. Chapter 8 looks at stories and what we can learn from thinking in fields as diverse as drama, persuasive communication and marketing. There is guidance on use of social and general media and advice from journalists, as well as sections on blogging and using visuals. Chapter 9 looks at language, with learning on style, voice and tone as well as practical advice on writing plain language summaries. This chapter goes beyond normal style guides on good writing to look at the particular challenges for researchers in conveying complex findings in a clear way while avoiding over-simplification and 'spin'. The last chapter brings together reflections on how researchers can strengthen their findings by drawing on key lessons, insights and analysis throughout the book and stay relevant at a time of change and uncertainty.

There are some recurrent themes throughout this book. But one message is that researchers need to make strategic *choices* about the journey of your research into the wider world. Thinking carefully about how you do this will pay dividends. As a small example of conscious choices, in structuring this book I decided that the order of chapters was important. I wanted the WHO chapters to go before HOW – that is, think audience before format. In the HOW section, I wanted the chapter on stories to go before that on language – narrative should come before style. And it is clear that there is an interdependence in the chapters, so that questions of style should reflect the idiom, concerns and priorities of target audiences, whether they be a patient advocate or a hospital medical director. Without an understanding of your audience, advice on the best ways of communicating research findings will fall short.

Research or evidence?

A note on the use of the terms research and evidence, which are sometimes used interchangeably by many. But there is a distinction. Research is the output of scholarly, published work usually in peer-reviewed journals and academic books. Evidence is a wider term, defined by the National Institute for Health and Care Excellence (NICE) for their purposes as:

> Information on which a decision or recommendation is based. Evidence can be obtained from a wide range of sources, including randomised controlled

trials, observational studies and expert opinion (of practitioners, people using services, family members and carers). (NICE 2020)

This is a useful distinction, as it reminds us that research is only one part of the wider information needed to make decisions. A community health manager is perhaps more likely to speak to a local public health consultant or get improvement stories from care homes when looking for evidence to support service change. This is explored further in the next chapter, considering the 'what' of knowledge. But it is worth stating at the start of this book that researchers can think about how to transform their raw findings ('research') into 'evidence' which is useful to decision-makers, by understanding their audience, adding contextual information such as professional views and practice perspectives and using 'hooks' to engage interest and attention. An academic paper on its own is unlikely to make a substantive difference to policy and practice.

Learning from our evidence centre

This book draws on some of the approaches adopted by our centre, a national agency set up in 2015 to disseminate health research. Our activities were informed by some of the theories and understanding on knowledge mobilisation set out in this book, particularly in engaging stakeholders in meaningful ways to interpret research and develop our evidence products and activities. Using this bedrock of knowledge, and a steering group of experts, we developed and adapted approaches to making research findings relevant and useful for frontline staff and others. We learned as we went along, measuring use and reach of different formats and getting valuable feedback from the individuals and organisations we worked with, as well as some limited independent evaluation. Illustrative examples in this book highlight positive features which appeared to increase our relevance and reach, but not all activities were successful. At times, we did not get traction with professional or public networks on particular topics. In identifying opinion leaders with 'voice', we may have given priority to some disciplines and professions at the expense of others. More research is needed on some of the pragmatic approaches to engagement and promotion adopted and developed at our centre and by other bodies.

The work of intermediary organisations, whether research dissemination centres, thinktanks or evidence centres, has been given recent welcome scholarly attention (Davies et al 2015; Boaz et al, 2019; Isett and Hicks, 2020), some of which is discussed later in this book. But much of this is theoretical or organisational, with little emphasis on the day-to-day activities of engaging stakeholders and developing tailored research products. Davies et al (2015) noted the paucity of formal evaluation and systematic learning of approaches to sharing and promoting research taken by funders and intermediary bodies. This is an interesting field, with more evaluative activity and critical attention warranted. Until more high-quality empirical studies of 'what works' in engagement and dissemination practice become available, some of the descriptive examples of products and activities like those from our centre are worth sharing now.

Format and interviews

At the end of each chapter, there are practical pointers for reflection and actions to practise the craft of engaging and writing for impact. I have carried out interviews scattered throughout the book with leading researchers, journalists, scientists and communicators (see List of Interviews, p viii).

These 15 interviews provide helpful insights from communication experts of different kinds in how to tell the story of your research in the most effective way. I have also illustrated the book throughout with examples of research which has communicated well with target audiences and made a difference. Many of these are drawn from areas which I know best in health services research – particularly supported by the National Institute for Health Research (NIHR) – in the UK. But there are many other examples of innovative dissemination and engagement in other fields and countries. There is a real need to develop repositories of good practice and exchange learning on how to bring research to life for different audiences. There is much we know and much we have still to learn about what works in making research more used and useful.

2

WHY researchers should spend time on this

Summary

This chapter starts with a brief overview of where we are in the history of understanding how health and social care research moves into practice (or not) and why it matters, including the time taken for research to have traction. I consider the mismatch between research which is produced and information which decision-makers want. Increasing volumes of information of all kinds now make it harder for research to be seen. There is a short account of scholarly debates on the way in which research influences practice and how our thinking has changed, from researchers broadcasting findings to more nuanced understanding of the complex interactions between researcher and user working in dynamic systems. This matters because it informs the practical steps and tactics needed to get your research noticed and understood. The chapter ends with five general steps for better engagement, which are tailored for different audiences in later chapters. There are also pointers to broader bodies of work on impact and implementation, which overlap but extend further than the scope of this book.

Making sense of research findings

I was at a meeting discussing recent research we had summarised for ambulance staff and services on emergency care. The showpiece was a large randomised trial, one of the largest of its kind in an out-of-hospital setting, comparing mechanical devices with manual compressions in treating cardiac arrests (Gates et al 2017). The high-quality trial showed no real difference in survival rates between the two. Given the high costs of the automated devices, it suggested potential cost savings for the service. But discussion at this event became heated. Many of the ambulance trusts had already invested in the mechanical Lucas devices. Staff liked using them, feeling reassured by the equipment and – no small thing – feeling safer, as they could stay seated with seatbelts on instead of attempting resuscitation in the back of a jolting ambulance at speed. So the conclusion of many paramedics and managers in the audience was that, if outcomes were similar, they wanted to go on using the mechanical devices.

This was a valid interpretation of the research. But it came as a surprise to me, already drafting headlines for policymakers on potential cost savings and efficiencies. I had not realised that other factors, like acceptability to staff and use in the real world, might affect the way the research findings landed. It reinforced for me the need to understand what matters to different audiences. Without a knowledge of audiences and context, research will not matter to those making decisions on the ground. The same research findings can be framed and understood in many different ways. There is an art and science to presenting research well.

Understanding the different ways that research can be interpreted is important. And the role of the researcher guiding the process by which different audiences make sense of research findings and shape the outputs is a critical but often neglected aspect of academic life. Dissemination and promotion of research findings often comes at the end of a project when the team is dispersed and the contract funding has stopped. But thinking about who might be interested in the research or parts of the research and engaging that community should happen much earlier at the point of designing and delivering the study. Research which influences policy and practice usually has meaningful engagement with stakeholders throughout the study. It may take time to do this well, but is likely to maximise the relevance and usefulness of research.

At the same time, researchers need to contend with developments in information, technology and research production which make it harder (in some ways) for their work to be noticed. This chapter explains *why researchers should spend time thinking about how best to present their findings*. This includes an account of the competing demands for readers' attention and how in the past research has often seemed remote from the urgent demands of those making decisions. We know more from theory and research about the journey from research to practice and what strategies may help to connect findings with particular audiences. The recent turn in research policy and funding to give greater attention to external impact has intensified the need for researchers to invest more effort in getting their findings used by the right people in the right way. The chapter ends with general principles of effective engagement summarised in five steps which are worked up for particular audiences in Chapters 4–6.

What is the problem? Time lags, information overload, research waste

Researchers want their work to make a difference. Policymakers or service leaders want to draw on best evidence when making difficult decisions. And yet it is still very difficult for the right research to reach the right people in the right way at the right time.

Let's start with some numbers. It is estimated that only about 60 per cent of healthcare treatments are based on best evidence (Braithwaite et al 2020). Despite the machinery of clinical guidelines and other useful ways of structuring evidence for practitioners, there is still a large gap between research and practice. It is often said that it takes 17 years for research to embed itself in practice – a figure which is contested (Morris et al 2011), but still widely cited. There are varying accounts of different types of time lags, from drug discovery to commercialisation, from research publication to clinical guideline recommendation (Hanney et al 2015). But by any measure, it still it takes far too long. And adoption is uneven – there is now a whole evidence base on variation in proven treatments, with one study showing four-fold variation in different parts of the country for people getting effective treatments like hip replacements and cataract surgery, having adjusted for need (Appleby et al 2011).

There is much to be proud of in the UK, with pioneers like Archie Cochrane, showing the importance of systematically testing and synthesising evidence to drive best practice, leading to the development of institutions like NICE (Timmins et al 2017). The movement of evidence-based medicine, which in the 1970s was seen as disruptive and radical, has now become embedded in the NHS mainstream with high-quality pragmatic trials commissioned to address important clinical knowledge gaps feeding into national guidelines and standards. We are lucky to have a national needs-led research system and infrastructure in the form of the NIHR which delivered a world leading pragmatic trial on COVID-19 treatments in a matter of weeks. This identified a low-cost, widely available steroid treatment as an effective option, now taken up across the globe (RECOVERY Collaborative Group 2021).

For clinical and biomedical research, particularly trials looking at the comparative effectiveness of treatments, there are now well-established mechanisms for evidence to reach practice. High-quality trials, synthesised in systematic reviews, provide a foundation for clinical guidelines in many areas, from the management of people with stroke (Rudd et al 2017) to early intervention for young people with psychosis (NICE 2016). Other large-scale studies have had direct influence, such as the national prospective cohort study of outcomes by place of birth informing guidelines on intra-partum care (NICE 2017). For other kinds of research, such as studies looking at health service delivery, quality of care, patient and staff experience there are fewer systematic or nationally recognised channels for research to reach decision-makers. This means that researchers need to make more *active* efforts to package and promote their research for particular audiences in partnership with others.

Another problem is the sheer volume of information and research which is produced and increasing year on year. One analyst estimated that 40 years ago a mental health nurse or doctor might have needed to read three papers a day to keep on top of their field. Now it would be over 200 (Badenoch and Tomlin 2015). In the broader field of biomedical sciences, over two million articles a year are indexed in PubMed database every year, landing at a rate of around two papers a minute (Landhuis 2016). And much of this is of questionable quality. Alvesson et al (2017) in a lively polemic give examples of how current incentives in the academic system are leading to overproduction of research which is 'meaningless'.

Although contested as a measure of value, one crude measure relates to the number of times a paper is referenced in scholarly work. It is estimated that about a third of social science papers never get cited even once by other researchers (Larivière et al 2009). Such measures may be flawed – for instance, another analysis of 'never cited' organisational research using standard databases found they overlooked references in books, online journals and repositories (Prichard 2013). And a more important limitation is that the number of times a paper is cited and used in scholarly work should not be equated with its usefulness or worth. Indeed, over-reliance on bibliometrics is now giving way to a turn towards more responsible research metrics (Wilsdon 2017).

However, such figures still raise questions for the research community. Perhaps the most startling statistic of all was an estimate ten years ago by scholars that 85 per cent of all published health research may be flawed, due to problems of incomplete reporting, poor study design or execution (Chalmers and Glasziou 2009). We will never know an exact figure for the quality and value of all health and social care research. But we do know that too much research in the past was answering the wrong questions in the wrong way, took too long or never reached practice.

It has also become more difficult for readers to find relevant, high-quality research in an avalanche of information. The next chapter, looking at what counts as evidence, considers in more detail how research outputs sit in a world of expanding information, channels and journals. There are many positives to the opening up of data, with new kinds of information more accessible to many. But it also makes it more difficult for research to compete with other kinds of information, some of which may be flawed or misleading. This problem has become amplified in times of emergency, such as the COVID-19 pandemic, where we are hungry for immediate information and it becomes more difficult to tell what is reliable.

The problems with research information – too much, too little, too late – are now well recognised. A series of influential papers on research waste, recently updated, highlighted powerfully the ways in which much research is of low-quality or addresses the wrong questions and what can be done to improve the rigour and relevance of what gets funded and published (Glasziou and Chalmers 2018). But the research itself is only part of the problem. We also need to look at other features of how research makes the journey to reach people who might find it useful.

From dissemination to engagement – how our thinking has changed

We can see development in our understanding over the last 20 to 30 years in how research is used (or not) by policymakers and practitioners. Some of this evolution is described well in a paper by Best and Holmes in 2010, with further refinements in a paper by Holmes et al in 2017. Although there are different ways of conceptualising the journey of research into practice, Best and Holmes (2010) describe a progression from linear models, to relational approaches to systems thinking. Different approaches may be appropriate for different kinds of research or circumstances, but we can also see these as evolutionary stages in our understanding of how evidence influences policy and practice.

Early work assumed a rational, *linear* model in which research is seen as a 'product' which stays the same whatever the audience or context, which can be pushed or promoted to end users in a one-way direction. These users were in essence passive consumers of research they received. This model also assumes direct and immediate impacts from the moment of publication, with influence through a chain of predictable steps. The focus for researchers was on effective communication and dissemination of their work.

In the next *relational* stage of thinking, evidence use depends on good relationships and processes. This involves understanding by researchers of the networks and communities of practice of people they are trying to reach. It often links to the work of individuals who can span or mediate the different worlds of research and practice, acting as knowledge brokers. Many research bodies or collaborations now employ individuals who combine research understanding with backgrounds as clinicians or professionals to better promote research and frame it in ways that are useful to services and decision-makers.

The final *systems* model described by Best and Holmes (2010) draws on wider thinking which recognises that we live in complex and unstable environments, with different parts of the system interacting with each other in complicated and unpredictable ways. Systems thinking has become a useful paradigm in public health in thinking more holistically about wicked problems, from knife crime to child obesity (Rutter et al 2017). For knowledge to influence individuals or organisations, researchers need to understand the complex mechanisms, culture and context of the dynamic system. This involves understanding the roles, actions and drivers of different stakeholders and how they interact. In this model, researchers might need to look for 'occasions of influence' in a complex web of relationships and institutions, a theme I pick up later in chapters on policymakers and timing of research.

This useful evolutionary model has some overlap with earlier thinking, such as influential work by Jonathan Lomas (Lomas 2000) among others on differences between models of *push* (in which researchers produce research and broadcast to the world), *pull* (where researchers respond to the needs of decision-makers and create a demand for their work), to *linkage and exchange* (the approach of collaboration and shared learning between researchers and end users). Graham and Tetroe (2007) conceptualised a circular model, showing the need for feedback loops and interaction between researchers and users in dynamic ways.

This wider lens extends to discussion about what constitutes an effective 'evidence eco-system' (Boaz and Nutley 2019), looking at interconnected elements which may include research funders, institutions, journals, clearing houses and intermediary bodies as well as the individuals and organisations using evidence. This acknowledges the complexity and interactions in a system of research generation and use – a long way from traditional notions of research pipelines.

In the many conceptual frameworks and debates on evidence use, I find perhaps the most helpful is one developed recently by Mark Rickinson and colleagues for schools and education, based on a wide survey of relevant literature from different settings on effective evidence use. This has as its centre two organising principles of appropriate evidence coupled with thoughtful engagement and implementation. These depend on different enablers for individuals (skillsets, mindsets and relationships), organisations (leadership, culture and infrastructure); and broader system-level influences (Rickinson et al 2020). This acknowledgement of the complex, multiple levels of activity and influences, together with the core principles of finding evidence which is relevant and developing careful strategies to reach audiences, resonates with my experience of what works in effective evidence use.

Let's talk about impact

Since 2014, impact on wider society has formed a substantive part of the way in which the value of research is assessed by the four UK higher education funding bodies. This marks a shift from a model in which the main measures of success centred on academic recognition, from awarding of grants to how many times papers were cited or appeared in a handful of high-status journals. The Research Excellence Framework (REF) in 2014 marked a departure in the way quality was assessed in universities. Researchers put forward case studies for review by expert panels which demonstrate impact. This is defined as 'an effect on, change or benefit to the economy, society, culture, public policy or services, health, the environment or quality of life, beyond academia' (REF2021 2019). These impact case studies or stories are important. In 2021, the assessment of external impact makes up a quarter (previously a fifth) of the score on which decisions are made about allocating funding of the block grant between universities.

But although these system incentives have fuelled greater interest in the real-world difference that research makes, the practical steps which researchers can take to maximise the influence of their findings are often not clear. An analysis of 162 health-related impact case studies in an earlier round in 2014 (Greenhalgh and Fahy 2015) showed that most submitted evidence focused on linear accounts of how research reached practice, relying heavily on trials with clear pathways to practice influence through mechanisms like clinical guidelines. The more sophisticated understanding of the diffuse and complex ways in which research informs practice, outlined earlier in recent scholarly debate about systems thinking in research journeys, was not evident in the majority of these case studies. The authors in this study noted 'researchers' relatively low emphasis on the processes and interactions through which indirect impacts may occur'. Less than a quarter of the case studies described targeted knowledge mobilisation activities in any detail or the active steps to achieve influence.

Given the interest in impact by researchers and universities, an important new body of evidence has emerged investigating research impact itself. A good starting point to understand some of this scholarly debate is the overview by Katherine Smith and colleagues on how impact is measured and (ironically) the impact of this shift in focus on research and researchers (Smith et al 2020), a theme also taken up by Tina Haux looking at different dimensions of impact in social policy research (Haux 2019). This is a growing field of inquiry – a quick scan of Google Scholar shows over 1,400 published academic articles on research impact in the last six years. Contributions range from practical tips on preparing impact case studies, such as Mark Reed's handbook drawing on his own examples of agrifood research (Reed 2018) or the comprehensive guide by Patrick Dunleavy and Jane Tinkler (Dunleavy and Tinkler 2020) on maximising academic input and profile, which includes an introduction to the new sciences of tracking reach and use including social media, a field known as *altmetrics*. This goes beyond traditional citations in academic journals to include a portfolio of web-based measures including mentions in newspapers, blogs, Twitter and feeds into policy and discussion. This is still an emerging science, with a recent review noting that 'initial studies suggest that social media has rather opened a new channel for informal discussions among researchers, rather than a bridge between the research community and society at large' (Sugimoto et al 2017). However, becoming fluent in the new language of social media and understanding how to craft online professional and personal identities, are likely to be increasingly important skills for researchers and are discussed in more detail later in this book.

As well as a growing body of work on measuring research impact and reach, there is also a large and complex base of research from different disciplines on how knowledge is translated or implemented into practice. This is described in different terms, from knowledge mobilisation to implementation science. Trish Greenhalgh provides an overview on this growing field looking at frameworks, tools and techniques for successful implementation and behaviour change, drawing on her own seminal work on diffusion of innovations (Greenhalgh 2018). Sharon Straus and colleagues (2013) provide a comprehensive academic guide to theoretical and empirical evidence in the field of knowledge mobilisation. The Further reading section provides a shortlist of books and articles I have found particularly helpful, for those who want to dig deeper or scan broader in related fields on impact and knowledge mobilisation.

Your strategy for engaging audiences

This book draws on some of these helpful wider scholarly debates on impact and implementation, but my aims are more modest and practical. I hope that this book will help researchers to decide how best to frame their findings so they are more likely to be read and discussed and used by particular audiences. It matters because public debate and understanding needs more than ever to be supported by reliable research. In today's busy world it is increasingly difficult for people to discriminate between different kinds of information and assess what is credible and sound. As a researcher, you therefore have a moral responsibility (Van de Ven 2007) to promote your work in thoughtful ways which will support better public understanding and informed discussion.

This book provides examples of research in health and social care which have made a difference, with insights from informants who are skilled communicators or influencers and understand the world of research. I have divided the material into chapters on what counts as evidence; who you want to reach – from practitioners to the general public to policymakers; how to maximise uptake by the right form and language; and how to anticipate times when your findings will have most impact. But cutting across these different audiences, formats and channels are some common principles I have identified for good engagement and communication strategies (Box 2.1).

Box 2.1: Five steps for better engagement

- ask the right research questions;
- understand the context in which your research lands;
- involve the right people throughout the study;
- partner with organisations, networks and champions;
- present content which is engaging and accessible.

Step one: ask the right research questions

For research to make a difference, it has to address issues which are important and relevant to target audiences. It also has to be designed in the right way to answer the question – a trial will not address questions of how services were implemented, and ethnography will not guide decisions about cost-effectiveness. Studies should build on what is already known in published evidence and address an important gap in knowledge. Research without appropriate or robust study design on a topic of little interest or importance to policy or practice will be of limited value. So the first principle of good engagement starts long before the study even begins. Stakeholders need to be involved in identifying important gaps and uncertainties. And when you communicate your findings, you need to underline why this area is important to particular audiences and what knowledge gap this fills.

Step two: understand the context in which your research lands

To make a difference, your research needs to be aware of the world in which your audience lives or works. A study on foetal monitoring would need to take into account the day-to-day working lives of midwives and recent maternal enquiries on avoidable deaths which may influence professional behaviours and system pressures. A project on recognising girls with autism would need to understand the range of professionals and pathways in schools, social work, healthcare and families who may affect timely diagnosis. Studies of homecare services and support for frail older people across the UK would need to understand differences across the four countries in funding and systems for personal care. To promote and implement your research findings, it is important to understand the drivers, incentives, culture and systems for audiences you want to reach.

Step three: involve the right people throughout the study

As a researcher, you may not be steeped in the world that you are studying. But you do need people with lived experience – as professionals or service users – engaged with the study as advisers or as part of the core research team. This is important to recruit and engage participants for the research but also to design the study which meets the core aims. Working with patients and carers on a hospice at home evaluation may highlight the importance of managing breathlessness as a tracer condition to be measured. Stakeholders can also help researchers to interpret findings, thinking about different cultural lenses and perspectives. Working together on research outputs will add to their relevance and appeal. You will also find out about where the people you want to reach go for information and the channels they use.

Step four: partner with organisations, networks and champions

It takes time to understand how practice and policy is shaped in particular contexts. You may not be immersed in these worlds. But you can make links with organisations or networks, from patient charities or advocacy groups to professional bodies, who have a deep understanding of your audience. Working with the right partner organisation can help you use the right language and find hooks which resonate with particular communities. They can also anticipate important policy or service initiatives and windows of opportunity when research can make a difference. Individual champions who have influence with a community can be important in reaching certain audiences and in successful social media engagement. Finding the right organisations and individuals to interpret and promote your research is critical.

Step five: present content which is engaging and accessible

In an age of information overload, the research outputs you develop for non-academic audiences have to compete with entertainment features and channels. This does not mean compromising the science or integrity of your project, but you do need to think carefully about how you tell the story of your research in different ways. Not everyone needs the full monograph or detailed information on methods and study design. Find examples and personal cases which bring to life your main line of argument. Work out how to summarise your findings in a headline or a tweet. If your resources allow, experiment with new formats from animations to podcasts. Write a feature article with influential leaders in a service-facing journal. Then use analytics and reflect with others on what approaches worked best to reach the right people, start a conversation and change practice.

These five steps are fleshed out for each of the particular audiences in Chapters 4–6. For instance, there are sections in each of these chapters on products which may be particularly appropriate to that audience. This includes feature articles in practice journals to reach frontline staff; plain language summaries for general public, patients and service users; and the policy brief for policymakers and managers. Although these formats may also be useful to others, they illustrate the need to tailor content and form for particular audiences. These chapters are followed by more detailed advice on telling the story of your research, finding hooks to engage people and using general and social media. There is also guidance on using language effectively and developing your own style. First though we need to consider the research findings themselves – or *what* it is that is being promoted and implemented. The next chapter considers how research sits with other sources of information that influence decisions and decision-makers of all kinds.

3

WHAT counts as evidence

Summary

It is not always obvious what is seen as valid evidence. Different stakeholders have different needs and value different kinds of information. This might include surveys, local health needs information, general media coverage as well as published research. Even for published research, it is not always easy to judge what is most reliable or relevant. This has become more of a problem with the exponential increase in scientific and other outputs, accelerated by trends towards Open Access publishing. Readers need help to filter and prioritise the evidence which is of most value to them. At our evidence centre, we did this with a community of people working and using health services who told us what research mattered to them. Researchers need to involve their target audience at all stages of their projects to ensure their research stays relevant to their readership. Early engagement will help to stay focused on the problems and outcomes that matter to that audience and to understand the ways in which they might make sense of the findings. This will help to translate formal academic knowledge into evidence which will support and inform everyday practice. There are insights on making your research inclusive and reaching diverse audiences.

Different kinds of evidence

It seems obvious what we are talking about when we are talking about evidence. It is published research, right? Not always. Evidence means different things to different people. And asking for the 'best evidence' or 'most relevant evidence' may end up with very different kinds of information, depending on who it is for and the nature of the question. Let's take just one example – social prescribing (Box 3.1).

Box 3.1: Research example – social prescribing

Just what the doctor ordered

Social prescribing has been widely promoted and adopted in the NHS, most recently in the Longterm Plan in England (NHS 2019). This is a general approach where general practitioners (GPs) or other health staff can refer patients with complex needs or problems to a range of non-clinical services. This is usually done through a link worker and may include walking clubs, art classes or befriending schemes often run by voluntary and community organisations. Given that many people presenting to GPs have longstanding problems not easily translated into treatment solutions, and our growing understanding of the social and wider determinants of health, this seems self-evidently a good thing.

But in terms of what difference it makes, the evidence is mixed. A comprehensive review of UK-relevant literature in 2017 (Bickerdike et al 2017) found only 15 evaluations of social prescribing activities, of low-quality and high risk of bias. This review highlighted the complex nature of the intervention, with differing objectives from improving physical and mental wellbeing to reducing use of GP and other services. There are no current evidence-based national guidelines for their use.

Interestingly, a realist review on social prescribing has since been published (Tierney et al 2020). This drew on a large range of UK-relevant material, including grey literature and local evaluations from commissioning authorities, to draw up programme theory to explain the kinds of features which need to be in place for link workers to be effective. This approach which pays less attention to methodological quality of individual studies, as even uncontrolled before-after studies may usefully describe features of schemes, helps to identify mechanisms of success. This includes the 'buy-in' and relational connections of link workers within their local communities which are conditions for success of such complex schemes. In this case, the 'what' of evidence is closely aligned to the 'how' of study design and methodology. A formal systematic review would only have included randomised trials. This realist review embraced a range of evidence for a different purpose.

What interests me is not just the paucity of evidence for this new approach which has been adopted so enthusiastically in policy and practice, but thinking about social prescribing also shows the variety of evidence which different people might want. From the GP perspective, the most important question might be – which of my many patients presenting with non-specific or complex problems would be most likely to benefit? And which schemes are most likely to be effective in terms of improved outcomes? For the local commissioner of services, it might be which of these activities are most cost-effective and what data is there locally on provision, uptake and resources. And how can we best recruit, support and retain link workers or navigators? Individual patients might want to know what it is like to join a healthy eating cooking class, did people enjoy it and what made them stay? A local advocacy group for people with learning disabilities might want to know how these services are funded and their fit with other statutory and voluntary services in their patch. And at a national policy level, as well as questions of cost-effectiveness, there may be an appetite for 'good news' stories to satisfy ministers and Treasury officials as part of the story of the policy on universal personalised care.

These are all different questions demanding different kinds of evidence. Evidence could include controlled before-after studies of particular social prescribing initiatives but also mapping data on availability and use of local services, descriptive case studies with quotes from referring staff, patient diaries and videos.

The case of social prescribing evidence shows that the 'what' is not straightforward. This struck home with me in an exercise some time ago when I carried out a series of recorded interviews with leading health service leaders. I naively asked each of these individuals with distinguished careers as top managers to name a health service research study which had influenced them. They were stumped (luckily, not live broadcast). After a bit of gentle prompting from me, a few came up with some of the management theorists fashionable at the time, from Clayton Christensen on disruptive innovation (Christensen 2013) to Michael Porter on value chains (Porter 1985). The work of academic health services researchers was not mentioned. This was confirmed by a research study of NHS general managers who ranked academic journals as the very lowest source of influence (Dopson et al 2013). This contrasts perhaps with a clinical leadership culture which is more closely aligned with biomedical or health services research. I was struck at patient safety events over the years at how many senior medical and nursing leaders appeared fluent and conversant with the complex and nuanced work of leading scholars like James Reason or Mary Dixon-Woods. In Chapter 6, I will discuss some of the differences between clinical leaders, largely embracing evidence-based healthcare cultures, and general managers who come from a different tradition. As Walshe and Rundall (2001) note, these are different audiences with different resources and notions of what counts as evidence:

> Overall, the tightly defined, well-organized, highly quantitative and relatively generalizeable research base for many clinical professions provides a strong and secure foundation for evidence-based practice and lends itself to a systematic process of review and synthesis and to the production of guidelines and protocols. In contrast, the loosely defined, methodologically heterogenous, widely distributed, and hard-to-generalize research base for healthcare management is much more difficult to use in the same way. (Walshe and Rundall 2001: 443)

Understanding the expectations and cultures of your audience around research and evidence is important when framing your findings to address particular needs.

Make it relevant

It has become a bit of a tired notion to talk about the chasm between research and practice. But it is salutary to read through reviews of research in the company of a busy practitioner or manager. It begs the question of 'so what?' All too often, a systematic review will conclude that there was little evidence of quality on a particular question and more research is needed. Reviewers favour precise, narrow research questions with pre-specified outcomes and parameters in searches which can be replicated by others. This is important in the interest of building up reliable and trustworthy science. But all too often the research that is found is not answering the question that the decision-maker wants to ask.

One of the achievements of research systems, like the NIHR in the UK, was to set up systematic processes to ask stakeholders about the most pressing uncertainties in a particular area and to fund research to answer these questions. This complemented more traditional forms of grant-giving where renowned researchers came up with good ideas to further knowledge and made the case for their project being funded. I support one of NIHR's national research programmes on delivery and quality of services which identifies priorities for new research from stakeholder workshops, surveys and meetings with clinicians, managers, patients and charities. This gave rise to new research in particular areas of uncertainty, from studies to improve 24/7 care to evaluations of joined-up health and care services for the homeless.

Without a steer from the decision-makers in health and social care, there is a risk that published research is not relevant to real problems and practice. This is the first pillar of research waste, identified by Glasziou and Chalmers (2018). There is little value in a high-quality, reliable randomised trial of a technology which is not likely to be used. The first step in ensuring the value of research is asking questions which are important to clinicians and patients (Box 3.2).

Box 3.2: Research example – protective clothing

Will it keep me safe?

Asking the wrong question or the right question in the wrong way is a common issue with research. During the COVID-19 crisis, I passed on a rapid review that had just come out of qualitative research on barriers and enablers to staff adherence to infection control measures (Houghton et al 2020) to a friend who was working as a clinician on high dependency wards with affected patients. It seemed a topical and helpful subject, with a useful focus on staff experience. But to her it was not helpful. The review found 36 papers from different countries, in different healthcare settings and came to some rather general conclusions that adherence depended on training, availability of protective clothing, trust in the organisation and so on. My friend had more specific concerns. She hadn't been properly fit tested for a face mask. The discomforts of wearing hot, sweaty, restricting protective equipment had been minimised at the start. There had been some confusion about supply and inconsistent advice on changing of scrubs. The issues she felt were very different in different clinical settings, from intensive care to general practice which had been combined together in this review. In short, she did not get any new insights or resonance with her lived experience from this research.

This is not a criticism of the review. It presented fairly and accurately the published research which met the search criteria. But until enough high-quality observational or other research capturing lived experience of patients and staff on infected wards can be added to the evidence base, formal literature reviews are likely to fall short of decision-maker needs.

The right kind of research needs to be funded to answer questions about most appropriate and effective solutions. But also in formulating and understanding the problem, a wide range of information can be helpful. In the case of protective equipment, more informal sources from staff surveys to free-text content analysis of WhatsApp exchanges, might have generated more immediate and vivid examples of the problem.

More pragmatic approaches to rapid testing and evaluation can generate usable findings of solutions, although it is important to understand the weight of evidence and the extent to which single studies can address questions of 'what works?'

Timing is key and a policymaker, union leader or health professional wanting to know urgently what matters to staff, which infection control strategies seem most robust may find that available published research does not have all the answers. Academic discussion of what counts as 'good enough' evidence in areas like face coverings have become part of national discourse in the current pandemic crisis (Greenhalgh et al 2020). Who knew that arcane and scholarly debate on different methodologies and paradigms would be so widely aired in viral discussion of trials of face coverings or vitamin D? It will be interesting to see if these discussions reflect a turn in public understanding of the complex nature of the many kinds of research and evidence which influence policy and practice.

Relevant to whom?

In thinking about generating new knowledge and what is produced, researchers need to be aware of who might be excluded or not heard. There are many ways in which research may reinforce existing patterns of behaviour or information which are unfair or unjust. To take one example, historic failure to record ethnicity in routine data has led to gaps in what we know about inequalities in access or outcome of services for certain groups (Public Health England 2017). It may seem difficult and costly for researchers to reach more marginalised communities to take part in research. Studies which focus on excluded groups, whether they are young offenders or recent immigrants, may be seen as high-risk in terms of delivery against recruitment targets and study milestones. But there are positive steps that can be taken by researchers, identified in a recent conversation I had (Box 3.3) with a researcher leading work on underserved communities and disadvantaged groups.

Box 3.3: Interview – Ghazala Mir

Thinking about inclusion in research

Ghazala Mir, based at the University of Leeds, has a longstanding research interest in health and social inequalities. Historic inequalities have been brought into sharp relief recently by the pandemic and Black Lives Matter movement. It is everybody's business, and Ghazala spoke to me about the kinds of things researchers should think about to address issues of diversity and inclusion.

Hard to reach?

People often feel overwhelmed when thinking about equity and inclusion and how to go about it in the right way. But in fact we know a fair amount from research already about best practice (Mir et al 2013). It's partly having a different mindset – people talk about groups being hard to reach, but it depends on what your normal networks are. We all have our life experience, circles of influence and social networks. You can be mindful of the kinds of perspectives you have on your study team and advisory groups. You may not cover all bases, particularly if your research is wide-ranging, but as a research team you should expect to represent at least some of the populations you are studying in some way.

Start with the right question

Make sure your research is inclusive from the start. Is the research question relevant – Ghazala leads a large network in Leeds which brings together policymakers, practitioners, service users and voluntary organisations to work out what research will make a difference in reducing inequities in public services. Having the input of people working in and using these services every day means the research which follows is important and collectively owned, not reliant on an individual researcher identifying a gap or following their own particular interest.

Engage throughout

It's also about how the research is done and who is in your research team. Participatory methods are important in sharing power. You need a range of perspectives in the wider study team to ensure buy-in. You may not be able to cover all bases, but you can identify some important target groups and work with trusted community partners and advocacy groups to reach them. You shouldn't be generating knowledge about people if you haven't got their voice in the process. Research about excluded people which isn't validated by them can actually be harmful or unethical. Participatory methods can build in an important sense of accountability to the people who are the focus of your research.

Don't assume you understand

Having people on the team who act as cultural brokers, with informal and personal understanding of particular communities, is important in areas like interpreting data. When making sense of interview data, you may misunderstand something when viewing through your own cultural lens. It is important to validate your findings with the right people and check out what you think you are hearing. Part of this is not treating people as a homogenous group – you need to understand how ethnicity intersects with other kinds of difference like social class, religion, age. Ghazala made the point that she has a minority ethnic background but is not an insider in every context, given her education and work status.

Tailor and test outputs

Researchers can also think about the way findings are communicated, investing effort in summaries, visuals and easy-read versions. Making materials easy to read can improve access for many people from minority ethnic groups, as well as people with limited literacy or learning disabilities. Think about the range of language and formats which might work best, as well as issues of language support throughout the study. Consider tailored events or products – for instance, Ghazala ran a separate workshop with service users to share findings from her research study on depression in Muslim communities, as well as involving them in a more general conference. Working with community partners can be very helpful in testing different versions and outputs with target readers and co-designing events with impact and reach.

Right kind of knowledge

A seminal study in the emergent knowledge mobilisation field has been the research carried out by John Gabbay and Andree le May of how staff in general practices used evidence, guidelines and other sources of information in their daily work (Gabbay and le May 2011). Their insights draw from more than two years of ethnographic research, a 'deep dive' into working practices and evidence-using behaviour. Through shadowing staff, observing team meetings, quality and audit reviews, interviewing teams and individuals over time they concluded that there was little use of published research or clinical guidelines in a formal, explicit way. Instead, knowledge was acquired through speaking to colleagues, trusted opinion leaders, patients and pharmaceutical representatives. Knowledge was laid down through 'mindlines' or 'collectively reinforced, internalised, tacit guidelines'. This included their own training and experience, advice and information from trusted clinicians in their professional network as well as memories of the 'last worse case' for their or neighbouring practices. The concept of mindlines as a way of describing the complex ways that different kinds of knowledge are used has spawned other studies in the field (Wieringa and Greenhalgh 2015).

Another piece of ethnographic research on the subject of what 'counts' as evidence is an early study on patient safety in the UK (Currie et al 2008). In this case, researchers observed surgical teams, department and hospital approaches to identifying and recording patient safety incidents. They concluded that many common errors and patient safety incidents were not counted as they had been normalised and 'seen as routine ... within the everyday context of care delivery'. This included failings due to organisational issues such as staff shortages or availability of beds. Doctors were often reluctant to acknowledge such latent risk factors, terming them 'organisational' or 'non-clinical' issues.

Other kinds of error were around communication problems, missing information at handover or on records. Again, these were often not recognised as incidents by medical staff in the same kind of way that rare but well-defined acts of error, such as wrong site surgery, were identified and reported. The authors concluded that 'a major concern lies with mediating problems around the nature of knowledge'. In other words, defining what we mean by error or evidence is itself an important question for people trying to make services safer or improve the quality of care.

Evidence then is not only the research findings themselves, but how it is interpreted and made sense of together with a range of other inputs. For practitioners this may be 'praxis' – the clinical or professional wisdom that comes with years of experience and is embodied as tacit knowledge (Van de Ven and Johnson 2006). For policymakers, this might be a sixth sense of what will play well with ministers or meet the concerns of elected members. Cairney notes:

> For scientists, 'the word evidence is synonymous with research', but for policymakers such as civil servants, it is 'more synonymous with data, analysis, or investigation'; 'evidence' will include 'gray literature, raw data', advice from experts, lessons from other governments, public opinion and, in some cases, anecdotal evidence of success. (Cairney 2016: 22)

I will return again in Chapters 4–6 to the process by which the reader makes sense of findings with and through their own communities of practice. But it is worth highlighting the different kinds of evidence which might be seen as legitimate by different groups of people, including what might be termed practical and research knowledge (Van de Ven and Johnson 2006).

One overview of published evidence on knowledge translation schemes provided three helpful groupings: 'does the knowledge arise from structured data gathering (empirical knowledge), is it from practical experience (experiential knowledge) or from abstract discourse and debate (theoretical knowledge)?' (Davies et al 2015: 35). The authors noted the lack of agreement in the literature or in policies and practice of knowledge mobilisation agencies, such as thinktanks or policy research institutes, about what is meant by evidence.

Assessing quality of evidence

I return to the opening question – what counts as evidence? And it seems clear that it may be many different kinds of information with some link to an investigation, exploration or inquiry (research). If we only want to promote 'high-quality' evidence, what does this mean? Let's think first of all about published research. In recent years, the model of academic publishing has changed almost beyond recognition.

In the past, the assumption was that quality was guaranteed by the gatekeepers, that is editors and reviewers of medical journals. We know now that flawed research has been published in good journals. And there is a growing evidence base on the flawed model of peer review for publication and funding research, since an early review found few studies in this area (Smith 2006). Many agree that asking three to five experts for their views on the soundness of methods, interpretation of findings and fit with a wider evidence base is helpful. This is a fundamental principle of science, with the norm of 'organised scepticism' in which emerging findings are subject to challenge and criticism by fellow scientists. But these opinions and decisions are often inconsistent and unreliable. The evidence base includes studies showing systematic failure to spot errors, agree on aspects of quality and the impact of cognitive and institutional biases which may make radical or innovative papers more likely to be rejected (Nicholson and Ioannides 2012). Indeed, an interesting if controversial proposition has been put forward that peer review should be replaced by a lottery system for all studies meeting a minimum quality bar (Roumbanis 2019). Given the capriciousness inherent in decision-making around publication and the time taken from completion of studies to publication – a matter of years, not months (Welsh et al 2018) – this does not seem unreasonable. So we know there are weaknesses in the current system. And this is important, as recognition and progression in academic careers still rests on attracting grant income and publication in high-impact journals.

In response to these challenges, disruptive models of publishing have developed at pace. Open Access is a general term covering a range of activities by which scholarly papers are available freely at no cost to the reader. This contrasts with traditional models of scientific publishing where papers are only available by subscription, usually through libraries. The democratic urge to make science directly accessible to the people has fervent advocates and has taken on the nature of a social movement. Open Access takes many forms, but includes models of pay-to-publish (associated at times with journals of variable quality) and platforms which encourage preprint papers, where review happens after publication. By 2016, over half of UK publications were Open Access (Hook et al 2019). This proportion will now be higher, with recent commitment from 2018 through Plan S (www.coalition-s.org) of many major research funding bodies in Europe to making funded work openly available. This trend has accelerated in recent months, with the COVID-19 pandemic seeing many of the most influential pieces of research appearing as preprint articles. There are interesting debates at present and the eco-system of academic and science publishing is changing at speed.

The explosion of research activity around COVID-19 has added to the growing volume and production of research – estimates in 2014 that scientific output doubled every nine years is probably conservative (Van Noorden 2014). This is amplified by the 'noise' of social media, promoting articles and threads of interest.

This adds to the burden for the consumer or reader. How to discriminate between good and bad research? What is worth reading? There is a responsibility on the researcher not to add to this information overload unthinkingly. We are all 'cognitive misers' (Kam 2005 cited by Cairney and Kwiatkowski 2017), looking for the least possible information to address our needs. Not every piece of research needs to find a wide readership. Some may provide a useful block or foundation for other research which can make a difference. This is partly about the status of single studies as opposed to syntheses of evidence. The issue of spin and over-claiming for single studies is discussed briefly in Chapter 9.

But it is worth underlining here that not all studies deserve active promotion to non-academic audiences. Some research will add usefully to the body of knowledge, for instance a scoping review which may set the agenda for future research or a methodological study to validate outcome measures. These are helpful for other researchers, but not likely to be of interest to wider audiences. Spending time in planning the wider promotion of research and engaging with networks and partner bodies is not always needed. Researchers have a responsibility not to 'push' research unthinkingly in a crowded market of health and social care information. Understanding what your research means for the intended audience and, importantly, who does not need to know, are important parts of the research planning process.

Box 3.4: Involving end users in finding research which matters

In our work in a national health evidence centre, we produced several critical summaries a week of recent evidence. We set up a rating system to help us sift out the most important research from a user perspective. We looked at a good spread of research outputs from major funders and a hundred top biomedical, health management and public health journals each week. We recruited a panel of over a thousand nurses, allied health professionals, doctors, managers, commissioners, public health staff, social workers, patients and the public. We adapted and broadened a model developed by McMaster in Canada who set up a panel of doctors to rate medical abstracts.[1] We kept our system simple, asking people on a six-point scale whether they thought the research was interesting, important and worth sharing. They weren't asked to consider the quality or reliability of research, as we had critical appraisal experts on the team who had already screened the papers using recognised quality assessment tools.

What surprised us was the richness and diversity of the comments and the value of different perspectives on a single piece of research. They told us not only what was important to them but gave us valuable bits of *context* about how the clinic was usually run and why this information might help with a particular area of uncertainty. This extra layer of sense-making is important, particularly for international reviews of complex service interventions where individual studies may take place in very different health systems. For instance, understanding the findings of nurse-led clinics would depend on the professional scope of practice, cultural norms and models of chronic disease management in different countries. A respiratory specialist nurse could help us judge what this evidence might mean for asthma clinics here. The comments from raters, such as the ones in Figure 3.1 on a study of models of end of life care, helped us not just to choose the best research but to add context on why it mattered to different staff and service users.

We cannot consider the 'what' of research apart from the 'who' or the people who might value it. We will see in the next chapters that the process of making sense of information also *creates* knowledge. Our rater panel (Box 3.4) was one approach to getting this engagement in a relatively high volume evidence-promoting process. Many research projects engage stakeholders – managers, service users or practitioners – in their project from the outset to make sure that the study is asking the right questions in the right way throughout. This attention to optimising the value of the evidence being produced will make later stages of promoting the research easier and better.

Figure 3.1: Stakeholders rating research on specialist palliative care

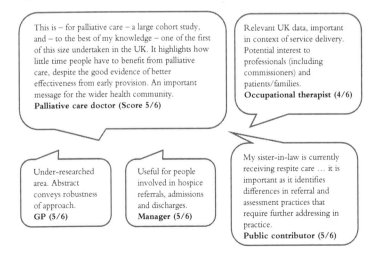

This is – for palliative care – a large cohort study, and – to the best of my knowledge – one of the first of this size undertaken in the UK. It highlights how little time people have to benefit from palliative care, despite the good evidence of better effectiveness from early provision. An important message for the wider health community.
Palliative care doctor (Score 5/6)

Relevant UK data, important in context of service delivery. Potential interest to professionals (including commissioners) and patients/families.
Occupational therapist (4/6)

Under-researched area. Abstract conveys robustness of approach.
GP (5/6)

Useful for people involved in hospice referrals, admissions and discharges.
Manager (5/6)

My sister-in-law is currently receiving respite care ... it is important as it identifies differences in referral and assessment practices that require further addressing in practice.
Public contributor (5/6)

PRACTICAL POINTERS ON WHAT COUNTS AS EVIDENCE

What kinds of information matter to your audience?

Find out what kinds of evidence are used by your primary audience by browsing practice journals, professional newsletters or chat forums. How is information presented and framed? For a manager, this might mean extrapolating your findings at a locality level – if this was implemented in a typical area, it could achieve this number of reduced bed days, cost savings or fewer patient journeys.

Add colour and context to your research

You can enhance and enrich your research findings by finding related news items, patient stories and case studies which may resonate with your target audience. For instance, a musculoskeletal study on referral pathways for low back pain may be strengthened by accompanying interviews with physiotherapists using new triage methods and vignettes of patient journeys.

Passing the relevance test

As your study develops, keep in close touch with people and organisations who are good proxies for the audiences you want to use. Share emerging findings in different forms and find out what resonates and interests them (and why). Ask them what they think the main messages are and who might want to know. Frame your study findings around the original decision problem or uncertainty which prompted the research and be clear about the weight of your contribution and what we now know.

4

WHO you want
to reach – practitioners

Summary

This chapter looks at ways that research is used by practitioners and how this could be improved. Using the five steps of good engagement, it starts with examples of research which matter to frontline staff and considers how these might reach individuals beyond academic journals. This includes an account of shifts in scholarly debate and understanding, from linear models in which research is packaged and distributed in the form of guidelines and toolkits, to more relational ways in which practitioners might engage with research through communities and professional activities. It is not just about how practitioners use research findings but what that knowledge is, using practice wisdom to interpret research in the context of daily work. Rich insights are given from interviews with practice-facing journalists, social media influencers and those spanning the worlds of practice and research in nursing, physiotherapy and social work. The chapter ends with practical pointers for enhancing the relevance and use of your research for practitioners.

Step one: ask the right research questions

I once interviewed some health leaders and asked them which research, if any, had changed their practice or made them think twice. One example given by a senior nurse was research by

Jill Maben showing that at the level of wards or clinical teams, high rates of staff engagement were associated with positive patient outcomes (Maben et al 2012). Put simply, happy staff equals happy patients. It helped this chief nurse to make the case for various initiatives to enhance staff wellbeing and team cohesion – from protecting space and time for ward meetings and debriefs to team social outings.

For evidence to be useful to practice and frontline staff, it needs to be the right kind of research which addresses real questions of importance. As Lawrence Green said some time ago: 'if we want more evidence-based practice, we need more practice-based evidence' (Green 2008). There are now mechanisms to set priorities which reflect practitioner and service user needs (see an account of the James Lind Alliance or JLA in the next chapter). The JLA exercise to identify priorities for social work research,[1] for instance, includes topics on eligibility criteria and thresholds, self-neglect and models of supervision. These reflect practitioner concerns and needs and should optimise the chance of research being read and used.

Box 4.1: Research examples – research which changes practice

In the past ten years, research has transformed practice in countless ways, from showing benefits of centralising services for patients with stroke (Fulop et al 2019) to the case for early intervention teams for people with psychosis (Correll et al 2018). Implementing evidence on infection control bundles, from changing catheters to identifying sepsis, has saved lives (Holmes et al 2015). More recently, the large-scale pragmatic UK RECOVERY trial involving several thousand COVID-19 hospital patients in the UK quickly identified a low-cost steroid as an effective form of treatment for those needing intensive care (RECOVERY collaborative group 2021). Research has the power not just to identify effective treatments but to save money – such as cheaper alternatives that work in treating wet macular degeneration (Chakravarthy et al 2013) to avoiding invasive shoulder surgery (Rangan et al 2015). There is growing evidence on effective interventions around families, from targeted home visits to new mothers to prevent child neglect to family drug and alcohol courts (www.whatworks-csc.org.uk). Research also shines a light on daily work practice, from intentional rounding in hospital wards (Harris et al 2019) to the emotional labour of healthcare assistants caring for older people with dementia (Scales et al 2017). And we understand more about the experience of people receiving services, from the work involved for people managing a long-term illness (May et al 2014) to the ways in which self-funders navigate the social care system (Baxter et al 2020).

Note that practice and practitioner here are a shorthand for the many and varied staff working in health and care, usually in service-facing roles. To name just a few in social care, this could include adult social care teams, family support workers, youth and youth justice workers, homecare service providers, voluntary sector staff as well as care home managers and staff.

Finding research which matters to staff (Box 4.1) is the first step to effective engagement. For instance, at our evidence centre we developed a review[2] of pre-hospital emergency care research, selected and interpreted with ambulance organisations and staff. This included research on clinical aspects of managing patients, such as use of adrenaline in out-of-hospital cardiac arrests, but also qualitative research on how paramedics make decisions on whether or not to convey patients to hospital. Identifying and prioritising research which had resonance for practising staff was an important principle of our thematic reviews. As mentioned in the previous chapter (Box 3.4), we also recruited a pool of over 1,400 raters, the majority of whom were health and care professionals, to assess recent research papers for importance and relevance. These helped us to prioritise research of practice value to work up as critical summaries which would be shared more widely.

Research which addresses critical uncertainties is necessary but not sufficient to change practice. There also has to be effective *mechanisms* to reach practitioners. In Chapter 2, we saw how Best and Holmes (2010) usefully conceptualised the three stages of knowledge translation. In this chapter, we look in more detail at some of these features in relation to practitioners. This includes linear models such as the use of evidence in guidelines to relational modes where trusted individuals or organisations reach out to practitioners, recognising a more reciprocal, two-way exchange between research and practice. Examples in this chapter which use more relational approaches range from knowledge brokers to online communities of practitioners or Tweetchats. The final systems model recognises the complexity of the world in which staff work. Embedding evidence into professional development activities is an example of one kind of system-level effort to encourage practitioners to engage with research outputs.

Box 4.1 gives just some examples of research studies which have changed practice and have resonance for staff, from senior practitioners in family safeguarding to community matrons to clinical lead radiographers. But busy frontline staff are unlikely to come across this research through papers in academic journals (Squires et al 2011; Renolen et al 2018).[3] They are more likely to see versions of the findings in news reports, practice journals, newsletters or online discussions as well as resources from intermediary bodies, from thinktanks to professional associations. This is partly about access but also about trust – emails or newsletter bulletins from a professional body are more likely to be read by practitioners than university press releases. Presenting the right information in the right way for practitioners is a skill. Eileen Shepherd, clinical editor for the *Nursing Times* has some good insights in how researchers can work with practice-facing journals (Box 4.2).

Box 4.2: Interview – Eileen Shepherd

Reaching frontline nurses

For over 15 years, Eileen Shepherd has been clinical editor for the *Nursing Times*. This is a practice-facing journal, with the most-visited website in Europe. Eileen shared with me many insights for researchers on what makes for a good article. She often works with individual academics to shape their work to fit with reader interest. Indeed, her top tip is for researchers to approach editorial staff at practice-focused journals like hers at an early stage. They want to receive good content, including stories or news coverage of findings which may have been published elsewhere.

The editorial team is happy to discuss if this is the right journal for the research and how they can support dissemination.

Eileen's first principle is to start with a pen portrait of the reader you want to reach – whether it is an experienced cardiology nurse, first-year student or nurse manager. The pitch will be different, but it is a good exercise to imagine speaking to your target audience about what is interesting about your work. This might take the form of a summary of your research or a news story, blog or opinion piece. If you are considering a blog, choose one critical finding or aspect of your study and expand in a conversational way. Social media is also a good way to promote interest and have a conversation with your audience about what your research means and how it could change practice. It is important to look at the social media reach of journals and how they could support dissemination.

The other way that readers come to research through journals is for learning opportunities, reflection and preparation for revalidation. Eileen points to the value of linking articles to online journal clubs and reflective exercises which all provide a great opportunity for researchers to engage with new audiences.

In terms of the kind of research which are of interest to frontline staff, Eileen notes the importance of evidence in areas of everyday practice which cause anxiety with potential for error. This might be around diabetes management or respiratory rate monitoring; a series of articles on respiratory monitoring saw a peak of 20,000 downloads during the COVID-19 pandemic. There is always appetite for new evidence in areas like workforce, patient safety and wellbeing, as well as content on essential nursing skills. Eileen points to good collaboration between researchers and journal staff in the shared interest of getting high-quality information to staff delivering direct patient care.

Step two: understanding context

Involving practitioners at all stages of the study helps to ground the research in the realities of everyday working lives. It might be important to place a piece of research in relation to existing service pathways or the ways in which care is normally delivered. Practice knowledge also helps to align findings to relevant policy incentives and drivers. This might include professional or quality standards, guidelines or organisational and financial constraints. In the critical summaries of recent research which we produced, we identified leading individuals to reflect on the implications of the findings for their practice. Contextualising the research against normal caseloads or clinics was useful in guiding the reader on what the findings might mean for them.

Understanding the context and ways in which research may reach practitioners is important. Three particular mechanisms and aspects are highlighted here. They feature the embedding of research in guidelines; use of research in continuing professional development activities; and wider debates on practice wisdom and how this experience is used to interpret and contextualise research findings.

Embedding research in guidelines

The last 20 years has seen increasing use of formal products and mechanisms like clinical guidelines as a way to get research findings into practice. The setting up of the National Institute for Health and Care Excellence (NICE) in 1999 was an example of a wider trend of new public management (Pollitt and Bouckaert 2011), in which rational decision-making and systematic use of evidence featured prominently. In the 1990s, politicians were under fire for 'postcode lottery' or inconsistent decisions by local commissioners on new and costly treatment, such as variable access to beta interferon for people with multiple sclerosis (Timmins et al 2017). The pioneer evidence body in health, NICE, spawned a set of What Works centres espousing similar principles and generating evidence toolkits and guidelines for decision-makers in fields from criminal justice to education to economic growth (Gough et al 2018).

The scope of NICE's guideline activity has expanded in recent years, from clinical treatment decisions in areas like managing chronic heart failure to broader work in public health and social care, such as multi-agency working in domestic abuse. The process of developing guidelines, with deliberative methods to assess evidence and use consensus methods to identify best practice with input from practitioners and service users, has itself become the subject of scholarly attention (for instance, Atkins et al 2013). It is recognised as part of a movement to codify knowledge into products and activities for organisations and individuals which can be tracked and monitored to ensure compliance with best practice and drive improvements, with guideline recommendations given statutory status in the UK since 2012 (see Wilson and Sheldon 2019: 78).

But there is growing recognition that guidelines are imperfectly implemented – Greenhalgh (2018) provides an overview of the theories and evidence to explain some of this variation in adherence (or indeed how it is framed as a problem of adherence in the first place). In Chapter 3, we saw how the 'mindlines' study (Gabbay and le May 2011) provided new insights on how practitioners use evidence. They described the social processes for practitioners in making sense of complex clinical issues, using coffee-room chat to check in, correct and adjust reasoning as part of a community in practice.

It is not helpful to think of the journey of evidence into practice as a rational, linear cycle or set of processes where nurses, therapists or managers articulate a problem, access formal guidelines or published evidence, appraise them and make an informed decision. The real world is not like that. This does not mean that research cannot influence policy and practice, but it does mean that researchers (working with others) need to make more active efforts to present, package and introduce their research into existing conversations and communities in the right way.

Box 4.3: Interview – Elaine Maxwell

Speaking the language of practice

Elaine Maxwell, former chief nurse of two hospitals and non-executive director of an NHS trust with experience in research and evidence use, talks about what is important. This includes framing research in the right way for your audience, including the terms people use and their real concerns. In many ways, researchers need to become bi-lingual – or at least work with translators – explaining research findings in terms that mean something to frontline staff or managers.

What do frontline staff need? Elaine returned to nursing on ITU wards at the start of the COVID-19 pandemic and noted the shift in what information she wanted and needed. 'My cognitive bandwidth narrowed and I could only take in so much information. I needed to get quickly to the findings and concentrate on the research which really mattered to me. I found the information and evidence around personal protective equipment (PPE) confused and confusing. There seemed to be little research in areas that were important to me, from the long-term effects of being on ventilators to the emerging pattern of "Long-COVID" condition.'

Researchers need to prepare their audience for their research and understand what the trade-offs and implications of results really mean. For instance, Elaine noted that a recent trial comparing standard mattresses with more expensive alternating pressure mattresses found no real difference. This was particularly important to nurses, who knew that patients often found the alternating pressure mattresses uncomfortable. This aspect was underplayed in discussion of findings (Nixon et al 2019), which focused on cost savings. She believed that stories of patients who couldn't sleep for several nights during their hospital stay because of the noise and discomfort of alternating pressure mattresses would have added impact to the (already persuasive) economic argument. You need stories as well as statistics, to engage hearts as well as minds.

Elaine urges early career researchers to get your name known – join in conversations online or in person. Ask to write a blog for the professional organisation you're pitching your research to, speak at their events or tweet about their conferences. Elaine knows of student nurses who have something to say who have gained profile and traction on social media and may be known to the chief nurse or nursing press. Social media is democratic, with little attention paid to formal roles and hierarchies.

Research as part of continuing professional development

A good way of making research useful is to embed it in activities like continuous professional development. Eileen Shepherd (Box 4.2) talks about online journal clubs and reflective learning resources on platforms like the *Nursing Times*. At our evidence centre, we identified learning and reflection points from particular pieces of research for practice sections of nursing and medical journals. These were questions which asked individuals to relate research-based innovations to their own practice and also review the strength and quality of evidence to develop research literacy skills.

In terms of continuing learning, Teresa Chinn (Box 4.7) developed an effective social online platform for nurses called WeLearning #AllOurHealth. This was a four-year social learning initiative with Public Health England to engage nurses in health promotion through topics like air pollution, cardiovascular disease prevention and mental wellbeing. The learning platform connected to Twitter-enabled discussion of latest evidence on a topic like tobacco control. There was a facility to record reflective practice on how individual staff used this evidence in their everyday work. This helped individual nurses chart their progress but also provided a powerful tool for researchers to demonstrate impact through the evidence journey and very small changes in practice. In Best and Holmes' third generation of evidence use, a systems model recognises the complex and dynamic structures and contexts which affect individual practitioners. (Best and Holmes 2010) Appraisal, revalidation and continuing professional development are important mainstream incentives and activities for most professionals. Placing research at the heart of these learning and improvement activities moves it from the margins to a more central place in practice.

Embracing the wisdom of practice

Our thinking about how practitioners use research is also informed by greater understanding of how knowledge is transformed in the act of being used. This contrasts with traditional notions of pathways of evidence into practice. As Green notes, too often there is an assumption of the practitioner as an 'empty vessel' waiting to receive passively the completed artefact of the research study (Green 2008). There is now greater recognition of the way in which the experienced practitioner selects and interprets research in an active process of sense-making.

This emphasis on the tacit or practical knowledge of the practitioner, which is seen as equally important as formal research or knowledge, is an important development in thinking about how evidence is used. It emphasises *praxis* or professional wisdom, acquired from years of experience and knowledge through doing. The principal social worker reading a paper on self-neglect or the consultant midwife hearing a researcher talk about risk factors in post-partum haemorrhage bring to bear their own experience when they process this information. Over 25 years ago, Hutchinson and Huberman (1994) used constructivist learning theory to challenge passive models of adoption of research in schools. They saw research use as an active learning process where teachers 'impose meaning and organisation on the disseminated information' they encounter. In this sense, practitioners could be said to generate new knowledge in an act of co-creation (Freeman 2007).

This is true for individuals and groups of practitioners. Indeed, there is an interesting scholarly thread on how learning is situated in practice and the social identity and culture of particular professional groups. In this way, knowledge does not sit outside these self-forming groups or *communities of practice* (Lave and Wenger 1991). In fact, communities of practice may be formed by the very act of 'thinking together' and making sense of evidence in relation to the work they do. This is shown in one piece of research looking at two communities of practice, one based on knowledge about dementia for occupational therapists and the second on sepsis-based practice for critical care nurses. This research explores how the self-governing groups came together and succeeded (or not) in providing a rich, informal forum for exchanging knowledge (Pyrko et al 2017). The idea of community being a crucial part of learning and knowledge-sharing is expanded further in the book, *The Social Life of Information*. This was written originally 20 years ago by John Seely Brown (then chief scientist at Xerox) but still prescient, wanting to return the focus to people and the relationships they form, rather than technology, in understanding how information travels (Brown and Duguid 2017).

Mary Dixon-Woods in an essay on context explains the importance of leveraging *practical wisdom* to successfully deliver and implement quality improvement programmes. She uses her experience evaluating the programme which saw a dramatic reduction in central line infections in over a hundred intensive care units in Michigan. This success was attributed to an evidence-based checklist with a bundle of care processes shown to reduce infections. But the evidence itself was not enough to achieve such results. She notes from her careful observational study of the improvement programme up close that many of the benefits came from 'creating a networked community structure that promoted social norms and shared learning' (Dixon-Woods 2014: 92). This included allowing flexibility for local units and practitioners to use their 'practical wisdom' to adapt the checklist – retaining core principles and standards – to align with the best of local custom and practice. An approach which exalted the checklist as an artefact, to be lifted and shifted to any environment, would have limited success.

In recognising the mutual and creative process of interpreting research for use, and the active part played by practitioners in filtering, applying and contextualising findings to their everyday work, the debate has moved forward from the idea of top-down transfer of knowledge to evidence which is 'collectively negotiated' (Greenhalgh and Wieringa 2011).

Step three: involve practitioners in your research and outputs

At our evidence centre, having selected studies which resonated with staff, we then worked with the people we wanted to reach to interpret and make sense of the research. We used the collective wisdom – and sometimes competing perspectives – of experts of different kinds to extract implications for practice. This might mean contextualising research for different contexts, for instance, considering what the effects might be in wards which were staffed differently from research conditions. Having multiple professional perspectives – as well as those with lived experience as service users – enhanced our work. For instance, a project on frailty involved nurses, physiotherapists, occupational therapists, geriatricians and others. When presenting findings, practice-facing outputs might have a particular focus. Staff often wanted details of particular interventions which were evaluated – how many staff at what grade and skill mix made up a virtual ward team? Was there a ward clerk? How many sessions at what cost?

Box 4.4: Using practitioner quotes and insights

'It can be very stressful for our crews to bypass a local hospital to take a critically injured or unwell patient directly to a specialist centre. However, ambulance staff are now better equipped with medicines, equipment and knowledge – and the outcome data shows that we are doing the right thing for our patients.'

Mark Ainsworth-Smith, Consultant Pre-Hospital Care Practitioner, South Central Ambulance Trust

---

Source: NIHR (2016) Care at the Scene: Research for Ambulance Services. doi: 10.3310/themedreview-000827

In our evidence reviews, we illustrated the report with quotes from practitioners involved in the project. They reflected on the impact of the research on their everyday lives – for instance (Box 4.4) a senior paramedic considers the impact of research and audit which has informed centralisation of stroke and trauma services in recent years, improving patient outcomes but considering how this feels for ambulance staff. We also worked with practitioners to ask reflective questions for targeted groups of readers arising from the research. For instance, a review of evidence on serious mental illness showed the benefits of starting treatment without delay for people with first episodes of psychosis. We asked readers, 'Do we know how many people with early signs of psychosis are waiting more than six months for treatment in our community?' The aim was to translate research findings into actions that could be taken locally.

Practitioners as researchers

In recent years, we have realised the importance of engaging practitioners – if they are a target audience for the work – in the research itself. The model of the practitioner-researcher is now well-established, with clinical researcher roles drawing on medical models now increasingly common in nursing and allied health professionals and social work (Shaw and Lunt 2018). These hybrid roles are useful in bridging the divide between research and practice. Linking to ideas about the wisdom of practice and tacit knowledge, practitioners as researchers drive activity which is centred on problems arising in practice. The processes of doing research and using the results are closely aligned. In some disciplines and professions, the strengths of practitioner-led research draw on approaches such as constructivist theories, where learners construct their own knowledge from interpreting their experiences.

I talked to Sui Ting Kong, a social work researcher who helped to set up a practitioner research network (Box 4.5). There is a spectrum of research engagement, from full participation as main investigators or co-researchers to advising on study steering groups. Models of participatory research enable building of relationships throughout the study which will help in sharing findings at later points.

Box 4.5: Interview – Sui Ting Kong

Involving social workers in doing and using research

Sui Ting Kong is an assistant professor of social work at the University of Durham, working in areas such as family violence. She talked to me about the interface between social work practice and research.

Her first message was not to privilege academic knowledge over practice knowledge – both should inform each other. That's why she helped to set up a network of practitioner researchers in social work (through the professional body, British Association of Social Workers or BASW).

'We struggled with our professional identity as a scientific discipline, because social work is a practising profession with a distinct knowledge base but not always fused with classic research traditions. But a turn in the last 30 years towards a stronger research culture in social work and social care has seen us realising we need to make research more practice-informed just as much as getting social work more evidence-informed. It has to be a two-way road. We have to force academics to forge knowledge with practice wisdom.

If we want to achieve impact, we need to involve practitioners in the production of research itself. We wanted to bring in likeminded research practitioners, set up a network, to think about new culture and new models of collaboration between research and practice. This helps us to build capacity for the profession to use and appraise research as well as take part in studies. At the same time ultimately what we want is to generate a new model of collaboration, providing a pool of practice knowledge collectively to inform research questions and practice-facing research. A very practical example recently was the way practitioners and researchers influenced a survey by BASW of practitioner experience of COVID-19, changing not just the way questions were asked but also thinking ahead on how findings can be accessed and analysed and interpreted. I have seen some exciting examples of participatory research hubs pairing academics with community partners, practitioners and families for instance projects on debt and poverty in Durham (Banks et al 2017).

We also want practitioners to engage creatively to develop or adapt scientific methods – innovation is important if we really want to democratise the process of knowledge production (and use) and make it more collaborative. Democratising is not giving up rigour, but challenging received methods, for instance looking at pragmatic trials in social work and issues like using wait lists as controls, we need the practitioner perspective to think about timing, the ethics and equities of this.'

Step four: partner with professional organisations and identify champions

In order to gain traction with particular staff groups, it is essential to work with formal and informal networks and professional bodies and communities. This is where practitioners meet, discuss new ways of working and receive information which is trusted. We engaged the Chartered Society of Physiotherapy early on in our review of evidence on musculoskeletal services in 2018. They hosted our first steering group, provided contacts (such as commissioners and specialist practitioners) and promoted and presented our review findings to their members, making up 95 per cent of the total profession. They also organised regional workshops to debate review findings for managers and practitioners developing musculoskeletal programmes and pathways and set up an implementation taskforce to support and monitor acceleration of evidence to practice. This included funding videos and patient-facing summaries of the review. They also provided a platform for promoting the findings through a popular physiotherapist podcast, with a reach of over 80,000 practitioners. Through their membership journal, the Society documented examples of evidence-led innovation such as physiotherapy-first clinics and new triage approaches in different parts of the country as part of the impact story.

Membership organisations and networks are powerful ways of engaging and promoting evidence (Figure 4.1).[4] But engaging with these networks and partner organisations early on is important to give you leverage and credibility with practitioners. You want to create the 'pull' for your research, rather than just broadcast findings at the end of a project.

Box 4.6: Interview – Godfred Boahen

Finding trusted intermediaries

Godfred Boahen, who worked as a research lead for the BASW, spans the divide of social work practice and research. Godfred talked to me about the separate tribes of practice and academia with their own language and culture. 'Academics need to understand the complexities of practice and the particular steps in the practice pathway where their findings might be useful. The more the researcher can do to tag their work in relation to particular work needs and practice pinch points, from safeguarding conversations to adoption assessments, the more likely it is to be used. It also helps if academics can specify who their findings are most likely to be relevant to, from teams working with people with severe autism to elected members with an interest in looked-after children.'

There is also an art in framing research in a way that will get the right attention – and may even change the conversation. An example given by Godfred is the acceptance of poverty as a core business of social work, a debate which was re-framed by research.

Most practitioners do not have access to academic journals. Researchers need to make use of trusted intermediaries, from bodies like SCIE in social work to thinktanks and professional bodies. And they may want to communicate directly via social media, although Godfred cautioned about particular ethical issues for social workers and others in using channels like Twitter when working in sensitive areas from adoption to safeguarding.

Figure 4.1: Working with partner organisations

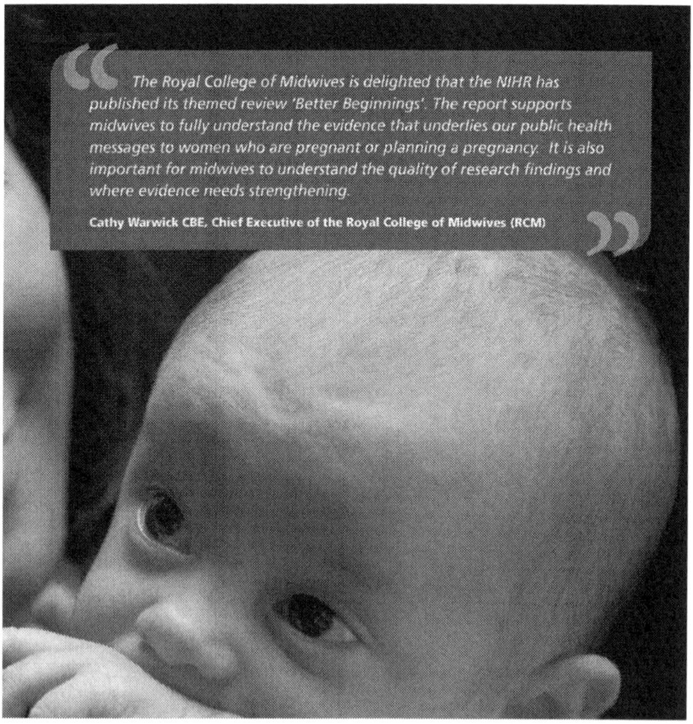

The Royal College of Midwives is delighted that the NIHR has published its themed review 'Better Beginnings'. The report supports midwives to fully understand the evidence that underlies our public health messages to women who are pregnant or planning a pregnancy. It is also important for midwives to understand the quality of research findings and where evidence needs strengthening.

Cathy Warwick CBE, Chief Executive of the Royal College of Midwives (RCM)

Source: NIHR (2017) Better beginnings: improving health for pregnancy. doi: 10.3310/ themedreview-001598

Knowledge brokers – practitioners as research champions

There are different kinds of influence and influencers. In work at our evidence centre, we tried to engage those with formal authority and profile, such as national clinical directors. But there were also individuals who were listened to and had sizeable numbers of followers on social media, although they may have been 'ordinary' practitioners. There is a science now of measuring influence, through social network analysis. This has been greatly used in marketing and other fields, but the basic premise is that you can chart relationships in a given community and identify those who are most connected and likely to influence others. Trish Greenhalgh, who has led work on how innovations spread, distinguishes between four types of influencer. These include peer opinion leaders – 'people like us and who we like' (my paraphrasing); expert opinion leaders – 'people we look up to in our world'; champions – 'people we trust who support an idea or cause'; and knowledge brokers – 'people who understand us and them' (Greenhalgh 2018: 187).

Knowledge brokers are typically employed to span the worlds of research and practice (Thompson et al 2006; Ward et al 2009; Bornbaum et al 2015). This includes the use of knowledge brokers in England's regional collaborations between universities and health organisations (Evans and Scarborough 2014). Given the different cultures and languages of research and clinical practice, these 'linking and bridging agents' need special skills 'to manage activity, enable interactions, develop shared spaces and negotiate tensions and conflict' (Rycroft-Malone et al 2015: 111). Over and above those with formal roles who are employed as knowledge brokers, every field has people with personal authority and influence who have service or clinical experience and understand research. Such people are critical in ensuring that professional and public debate is informed by research and in sparking interest and 'pull' for new findings.

At our evidence centre, we employed a number of clinical advisors, who combined knowledge of evidence with experience in clinical and service settings. This included a senior nurse with research background who was able to develop service-facing products with input from frontline staff on topics from frailty to ward staffing and host fringe events at UK national nursing conferences. She was also able to identify individuals with 'voice' and reach to champion our work, as well as engaging herself in social media debates and conversations. This included Tweetchats with nurses around evidence on ward staffing and care homes research.

As a researcher, it is important to identify the service opinion leaders and influencers in your field with an interest in research who can amplify and extend the reach of your work in relevant communities.

Step five: present content which is engaging and accessible

Using social media to reach practitioners

Just as hybrid practitioner researchers or knowledge brokers can span two worlds, there are also people with backgrounds in clinical or practice work who work as journalists or communicators. Newer social media channels provide powerful platforms to reach a greater number of frontline staff. I spoke to two leading influencers, Teresa Chinn (Box 4.7) and Jack Chew (Box 4.8), who have built up successful platforms for practitioners and are skilled in embedding research in everyday exchanges on social media.

Box 4.7: Interview – Teresa Chinn

Sparking connections between research and practice

Teresa Chinn set up the platform @WeNurses eight years ago – it now attracts just under 100,000 followers on Twitter and is a vibrant online community for nurses. Having not been particularly technology-minded, she joined Twitter to connect to people, feeling out of touch with practice news and developments as an agency nurse. This led her to set up an online network and forum to learn, share ideas, exchange evidence and practice tips. It is now a powerful platform for Tweetchats and active campaigns in areas from keeping staff active to raising money for nurses in crisis.

'I set up @WeNurses to fill a personal need to mix with other nurses, because I was working as an agency nurse, going from place to place. At the time, an agency idea of continuing professional development was to stick you in front of a video that was three years old, and I didn't feel I was learning or growing or staying up to date. Journals didn't really help, partly as I have dyslexia – for me, the experience of reading a journal is flat, I always learn best by talking to people. What I wanted to do was to connect with other nurses, discuss things that interest us, keep up to date and see what is new that we ought to know.'

Teresa Chinn, as a successful social media leader, has a number of tips. 'There's no point in crafting a perfect study, beautifully prepared with infographics and only sharing once. Be quite persistent in messaging, repeat throughout the day, perhaps with slightly tweaked or tailored tweets.' Like others, she points to the need for 'colourful content' – but, above all, to ensure that the headline message is clear. Also to frame research around the interests of the practitioner, keeping in mind what the audience needs.

Above all, Teresa reminds me that to be successful on Twitter you need to nurture and engage with your followers in a two-way process. 'It is all about reciprocity', not just broadcasting a message but responding to queries, enjoying the feedback and engaging in dialogue. And she urges researchers to 'get out there and share your findings' – although it may seem self-promoting, frontline staff want to know what researchers have discovered and there are people and facilities like @WeCommunities to help you get to the people who matter.

Box 4.8: Interview – Jack Chew

Physiotherapists in conversation with research and researchers

Jack Chew is a physiotherapist who set up his own podcast, Physio Matters, which now has an average monthly audience of 25,000. He was inspired to set this up seven years ago. In his own words, 'I was driving to work in Newcastle from Sheffield, a fairly long commute, and heard an Australian physiotherapy podcast, an interview with a great researcher on lateral hip pain, summarising her research and what it meant for practice. And I was a better clinician when I got to work because of this. Amazing. But later that evening, I clicked on to the next episode and I was furious, the guest speaker was a bit of a cowboy, saying things I knew to be demonstrable nonsense which were not challenged by the interviewer. In the space of the day, I realised the force of good and ill with this new medium. I was raging to my wife and she just said, why not do it yourself. So I did – I pick great guests, but give them a proper critical grilling – asking the questions you would ask as a physiotherapist, I am part of the audience.'

Like Teresa, he emphasises the two-way nature of a podcast, acting as a dialogue and exchange of knowledge and comment. The researcher can be in conversation with the practitioner (or proxy practitioner, as interviewer) and not just broadcast their findings.

His advice to researchers is to bear in mind the need to do more than inform. 'When running events, shows or podcasts, you've got to find a way of being entertaining these days – people are accessing this material, including scientific papers, in their own time. Don't spin or over-egg your findings, but make it interesting. Commuting, exercising, night feeds – that is when a lot of our audience are listening. So your work is competing with Netflix, Disney+, going for a walk with the family at weekends – not the *Annals of Internal Medicine*.' In the present age, an important rule is to entertain before you inform.

At our evidence centre, we spent time producing attractive, practice-facing reports with many case studies and stories to bring the research to life. This included for instance illustration of how bathrooms and kitchens had been adapted for older people with disability in a review on assistive technology. We consider in later chapters how design can play an important part in making research accessible. Our reviews also included quotes from frontline staff identifying aspects of research which resonated with them and how it had affected their practice. Feature articles, with case studies used in the research or vignettes of patient and staff experience, can bring findings to life. Using journalistic principles helps to make material readable and interesting, as many of the experts I talked to confirm. It is what Teresa Chinn (Box 4.7) refers to as 'colourful content'. But it is not just about the production values and adding a few stories. The key aspect underlined by many is the need to clarify the topline message and have a compelling line of argument. The more clarity you can get on your main messages, the better.

PRACTICAL POINTERS ON REACHING PRACTITIONERS

Know who you are speaking to

Draw a pen portrait of your target audience – it may be a district nurse in her late 50s or a community development worker in his 20s. Give them names, family backgrounds and interests. What aspects of your research would be most relevant to them? What recent service or policy changes might affect them and how can you add this context to your findings? What language would you use to appeal to them and what channels and sources of information do they use in their work and non-work lives? To get a sense of what drives and interests them, read practice-facing journals and newsletters. Go to a virtual conference or seminar, browse the abstracts and speaker backgrounds and visit discussion threads and forums online.

Map your stakeholders

Work out who are the important professional organisations and networks in your field of study. Identify individuals with influence in your world – these may be different for social media and other contexts. Who are the peer influencers, expert influencers, champions and knowledge brokers? Who are the gatekeepers to important networks and communities? What are the connections between these individuals and organisations? Understanding the chains of influence for staff in question can help you target your findings and strengthen your engagement.

Write a feature article

Plan a feature article in a practice-facing journal, drawing out the main findings of your work with a practice readership in mind. Use hooks of recent policy or practice initiatives which are relevant. Start with an arresting example from your research or a first-hand testimony of the problem encountered on the ward round or home visit. Use case studies of real localities where the approaches you are evaluating are being used and interviews with named staff, if you can. Test out your draft article with people who reflect the target audience, whether speech and language therapists or substance misuse nurses.

5

WHO you want to reach – patients, public, service users

Summary

This chapter will look at ways of presenting your work to the general public, patients and service users. They may be people who have a condition you are studying, look after a family member or are just interested in how services are delivered or experienced in their community. The first step is about grounding your communication in the problems which matter to patients, service users and citizens. This is illustrated by three recent research studies which are focused on topics of importance, from using emergency services to the experience of living with obesity to parents understanding risks of their children undergoing cardiac surgery. Understanding the context, priorities and realities of patients and service users is critical, with useful insights from interview informants. Research examples in this chapter all involved people in meaningful ways throughout the study, the third step of good engagement. This includes individual contributors who may be part of your team, but researchers looking to extend the reach of their studies need to also think about the role of organisations and networks. These might be patient advocacy groups, peer communities, charities and others. Using vivid stories to bring the research to life is an important last step of good engagement. There is general guidance on making findings accessible for public readers, including examples of easy-read versions of research reports, with advice in later chapters on using the media and writing plain language summaries.

Step one: ask the right question

Every research study starts with a problem or area where not enough is known about best services or care. It is always powerful when researchers trace the origins of their project back to the people and families who have prompted this study. This might be a project on improving oral care in care homes using an example of a resident with dementia refusing toothbrushing and experiencing pain, tooth loss and trouble eating. Research evaluating new forms of antenatal visiting may have arisen from the preventable death of a woman who missed booking visits and experienced complications. Or a study on digital befriending services prompted by awareness of social isolation experienced by older neighbours during lockdown. These are all examples of real problems affecting people where research might make a difference.

I have selected here a few recent UK-based studies which all have a focus on patient or public concerns and issues (Boxes 5.1, 5.2, 5.3). Each of these studies has something interesting to say about how people experience health or care. They have involved patients, parents and public consistently and thoughtfully throughout their projects. And they have presented research findings in interesting ways which will be meaningful to general readers, as well as academic audiences. These are just a few studies which caught my attention.

Box 5.1: Research example – use of emergency services

Why do people go to hospital emergency departments when they don't have to?

One study by Joanne Turnbull and colleagues explored the different ways in which people understand and use emergency health services (Turnbull et al 2019). This was partly in response to concerns about rising emergency department attendances with research suggesting some problems, such as urinary tract infections, could be better managed elsewhere. This mixed-method study included a series of panels and interviews drawing on mixed sections of the population, including marginalised groups (such as Eastern Europeans) and heavy users of emergency services in terms of very young and very old adults. It also involved a group of citizens and service users in the design and delivery of the research. This included getting people to draw pictures of where they go for what reason. This showed important differences in assumptions of those using services to those planning and managing pathways of care.

Researchers also used free-text from the qualitative research to illustrate key points, from interpretations of 'urgency' to thresholds for accessing different services.

> It might not be in their definition of a doctor's emergency, whether they can do something about it or not, if they're doing from a doctor point of view. But from our point of view, it's a panic. When calling 999 for my mum ... just being too floppy to get up ... It's not a sort of medical emergency, in their book, in their definition. But it is something that ... needs to be dealt with ... And it is something that is pretty concerning ... It's just that there's a sort of boundary thing, the definition. When we were living it, it's just being in a, sort of, very frightening situation. (Excerpt from qualitative text: with permission from Turnbull et al 2019: 51)

The researchers used this rich material to identify three kinds of 'work' which people seeking help do – illness ('what are my symptoms?'), moral ('can I justify calling an ambulance?') and navigational ('where can I go?') work. This draws on theories of the 'treatment burden' that people with chronic illness bear in managing and making sense of their illness day to day and making use of services and clinical support on offer (May et al 2014). This study highlights how few people understand the notion of urgent care (as opposed to emergency care) and the complex web of individual and community beliefs driving behaviour.

Figure 5.1: Testing displays of data for parents of children undergoing heart surgery

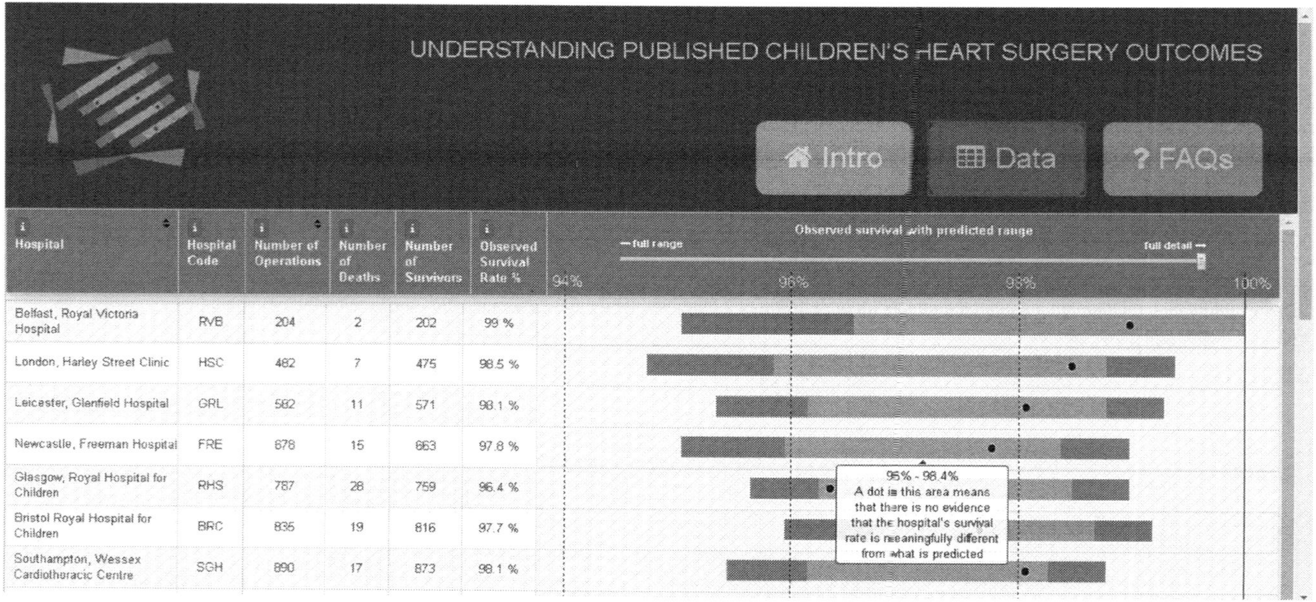

Source: Reproduced with permission from Pagel et al (2017), www.journalslibrary.nihr.ac.uk/programmes/hsdr/141913/#/

Box 5.2: Research example – how parents understand risk

Will my child do all right there?

Another study with some compelling patient-facing outputs was actually *about* how people understand and make sense of risk (Pagel et al 2017). This was part of a wider project on risks around children's heart surgery, taking into account other underlying health problems of children needing such operations. This had been contentious, as earlier work on 30-day survival rates after children's heart surgery led to temporary suspension of operations at one centre in 2013. This later study provided more complex models, adjusting risk for underlying health problems. As part of this research, an ambitious programme of work focused on the best way of presenting this new risk model to parents and the public. This was led by Christina Pagel (overall chief investigator) and David Spiegelhalter, a professor of public understanding of science, working with the organisation Sense about Science. Using eight face-to-face workshops over more than a year, they developed and tested different ways of presenting this complex and important information (see Figure 5.1). Four workshops were held with parents of children with congenital heart conditions who may need surgery or had had surgery. A further four workshops were held with press officers and staff from medical charities, hospitals and family liaison groups.

This programme of work included experiments to test knowledge about key concepts such as 'probability', 'risk' and 'predicted outcome' and many iterations of a website and animation. Parents and other workshop participants changed what was presented and how it was presented. This included the addition of important context, such as the need to emphasise that overall survival rates in the UK were high. Early versions had not been clear that hospitals should not be compared to each other on survival rates. And more work was needed on questions like what it means if hospital survival rates are below predicted ranges. Some important sensitivities surfaced. Original imagery to depict child deaths as black boxes were rejected by parents in place of a fade-out icon. Researchers and technical design staff worked with workshop participants to 'storyboard' content for an animation. This included simulation of 20 possible futures and answers to the questions parents asked, such as 'Is hospital X safe?' As the researchers state when reflecting on this sustained programme of work and interaction, 'there is no substitute for genuine co-production'.

Thought was given to the promotion and use of the website and animation. The website was tested for mobile phone and tablet compatibility. Promotion ranged from television and radio interviews, news and features in relevant charity newsletters and blog by a parent on mumsnet. It was widely promoted on Twitter and picked up by opinion leaders from Phil Hammond to Simon Singh.

Box 5.3: Research example – understanding obesity

How stigma about weight makes it harder for people to lose weight

Researchers Oli Williams and Ellen Annandale carried out some interesting research with people in a deprived neighbourhood who attended local weight-management groups (Williams and Annandale 2020). This explored the ways in which the stigma associated with body weight and size is experienced by individuals and how it may contribute to worse outcomes in health and wellbeing and more inequality. In a startling observation from their ethnographic studies of weight-management groups, the researchers coined the concept of the 'weight of expectation', people identified as obese or overweight actually feeling heavier at weekly weigh-ins when they judged themselves as falling short of ideal or socially acceptable levels of exercise or eating and drinking. These moral narratives of individual responsibility for healthy lifestyles were internalised and produced feelings of shame. The researchers described the paradox of body awareness. On the one hand, people of higher weights can be hyper-aware of their bodies – unlike those of lower weights who can 'forget' or be absent from their bodies, drawing helpfully on Leder's parallel notion of health and disease making people less or more aware of their physical self (Leder 1990). But on the other hand, people of higher weights in their study were often dissociated from the reality of their bodies, judging incorrectly when they had gained or lost weight.

Later, Oli Williams collaborated with illustrator Jade Sarson to create a comic based on these research findings about how weight stigma is felt in the body (see Figure 5.2). This was accompanied by a touring exhibition of the artwork as part of a broader social art collective, *Act With Love*, that he set up with his brother to collaborate with others and communicate evidence relating to social justice issues in ways that are accessible and engaging for wide and diverse audiences (www. actwithlove.co.uk). Together with his engagement through podcasts, blogs, magazine articles, television and radio appearances and talks at science events for the public, this is a great example of a researcher reaching the public in imaginative ways.

Why should anyone be interested? This is the first order question when thinking about communicating your findings. You need to draw a thread back to the original problem and connect it to the research which followed, using stories of individuals or families to make the point. In most cases, your research will have been funded because of some uncertainty or need which should be addressed to improve services or care. Sometimes you will be able to trace back to organisations or individuals who articulated the knowledge gap and why it mattered to them. Emphasising the relevance and potential use of your research to lead to better experiences of care is important.

Step two: understand the context

Researchers who want their findings to be read by people who may be affected by the condition or care in question, or have a general interest, need to appreciate a perspective that might be different from the professional or academic. A good understanding comes from close involvement with the right organisations and people with lived experience, outlined in more detail in the next section of this chapter. It also helps to hear the advice and insights of experienced people who span the worlds of research and public experience, like Sally Crowe (Box 5.4).

Figure 5.2: Comic book bringing to life research on weight and stigma

Source: Reproduced with permission. Artworks by Jade Sarson in collaboration with AWL.

Box 5.4: Interview – Sally Crowe

Dialogue not broadcast

Sally Crowe has experience in developing research literacy and making evidence accessible to patients and the public. She had three main messages for researchers.

1. Speak with, not at people

'There is a big push for researchers to get their findings out on social media. But there is a difference between "broadcast" mode and dialogue mode, although these are not mutually exclusive. What frustrates me is when a researcher comes with their findings to a community of interest, which is easy to find now with a social media hashtag. The researcher speaks, people are interested in the research, want to ask questions, find out more but the researcher doesn't enter into dialogue. It is all about developing the relationship.

I'm part of two social media groups: one for cancer, which I have, and one for "Long COVID" as I have had continuing symptoms. You can spot successful interventions by researchers when it is a dialogue and two-way conversation – there may be a request in there, perhaps to recruit people to a study or test out findings. Patients and the public have a healthy radar for spotting people who act as if it is a one-way relationship, extracting things without giving back. Researchers can learn a lot from sharing findings with those who might be affected, who might have interesting reactions to the research. Be open to what may come out of that dialogue with a patient group or community – let yourself be changed by the conversation, whether it is a different take on your results or ideas for further research.

2. Put the people back in

It's easy to forget the humanity in research – we may overly focus on methods, representativeness and reproducibility but it's ultimately people who make up the research, it is people who do the research. People take part in research because of an emotional response, for example they or someone they know has the disease. Very rarely do people come in from a public perspective because they want to know more about randomised controlled trials, but that's how the system sees it, thinking that's what people need to know. We need to focus on the human interaction, building on why people get involved in the first place.

When I'm working with different sorts of people in research understanding, stories and metaphors have proved powerful. Stories are not just anecdotes – evidence-based healthcare has sometimes had a bit of a problem with stories – it's an amplification of an experience which can embed and contextualise the research.

3. Don't over-simplify

People living with long-term conditions or life-limiting illness already experience lives that are complex and uncertain. My experience is that they can often cope with findings that are uncertain, that's part of life. People may not need over-simplistic tabloid 'silver bullets', I think what they want is honesty and transparency and a respectful way to deal with implications with their clinicians. Having said that, there may be issues of health and research literacy, particularly for people with cognitive limitations, or where English is not a first language for example. In this case, it is important to have clarity and simplicity, you need to land one key message.'

Sally has written a very good blog about how her recent experience of living with a rare and aggressive cancer has informed – and, at times, changed – her approach to engaging patients and public in research: https://blogs.bmj.com/bmj/2019/02/22/sally-crowe-patient-and-public-involvement-a-smooth-sea-never-made-a-skilled-sailor/

Step three: involve the right people throughout your study

Engaging public and service users in research

Engaging patients, public or service users throughout the study has become increasingly important but is not always done well. Indeed, there is a growing body of research on public engagement and whether it has led to changes in what and how research is done (Boaz et al 2016).

In the three research examples at the start of this chapter, the methods and outputs mirror the subject of the study itself. All are participatory and reflect the values and preferences of the patients and public who might be interested in the research. Having genuine input from people you want to reach throughout your study is an important factor in maximising the chances of it being used. And genuine input from public contributors can bring fresh perspectives on assumptions underpinning research and what it means (Figure 5.3).

Public and patient engagement has become a requirement for funders like NIHR in the research which they support. Levels of engagement vary, from a few representatives on a study group to public contributors as co-applicants leading parts of research. At its most developed, engagement becomes co-production where power is shared between the public, practitioners and researchers. This needs active commitment from researchers with 'constant reflection on power differentials and managing these to build trust' (Hickey et al 2018).

Indeed, there is a recent turn towards labelling everything as 'co-production' – so much so that a researcher recently coined a phrase new to me of 'cobiquity' (Williams et al 2020). There are real questions about what true co-production demands and how that sits with other aspects of academic practice (Oliver et al 2019). It is not easy to do this well, and recent helpful contributions have emphasised practical 'design principles' to thoughtful and effective engagement (Boaz et al 2018).

Figure 5.3: Service users making sense of research

> *I was interested in reading about the research on changing kitchens and bathrooms with special devices. But it made me think – why not make all designs disabled user friendly, so no adaptations are needed!*
>
> **Kate Brown, service user**

Source: NIHR (2018) Help at home – use of assistive technology for older people. doi: 10.3310/themedreview-03385

Engaging patients and the public in shaping the research agenda

An important development in involving patients and the public in identifying research needs is the JLA approach to priority-setting.[1] They have just completed their 100th exercise in which public members and charities or patient groups come together with clinicians and researchers to identify pressing problems which need to be researched. There is then a structured process with careful facilitation to prioritise research topics, ensuring everyone's voice is heard. There are various iterations to arrive at a top ten of the most important research questions to go forward to funders, although the translation of priorities to research is not a given (Staley et al 2020).

This deliberative process is well-documented, with a manual now in its eighth edition which has evolved since the first exercise in 2004 (Cowan and Oliver, 2021). The scope of the exercises has also broadened, from initial narrow treatment questions on effectiveness to broader uncertainties about experiences and services in areas like living with hearing loss and social work research. The genuine involvement of users has resulted in different research agendas than those set in traditional ways – for instance, the inclusion of breathing exercises in the top priorities for asthma research. This is an interesting model and it is noted that the strength of the partnership itself, bringing together stakeholders in a different way, is as important as the artefact of the priority list (Staley et al 2020) and could provide a powerful 'pull' for use of the completed research.

These exercises in involving and working with service users, patients and the public in identifying research needs, carrying out the work and sharing findings are welcome. But researchers need to be mindful of the complexities and the wider issues at stake. There is an established body of evidence, both theoretical and empirical, on the limitations of much public engagement, including failings in reflecting and reaching diverse communities (Ocloo and Matthews 2016). Peter Beresford has worked for many years in the fields of public engagement and advocacy, rooting his work in a deep understanding of wider contexts (Box 5.5). This includes both the political, institutional and structural forces at play and the broader movements of civil rights and identity which inform many of the challenges and blocks to meaningful engagement (Beresford 2016).

Box 5.5: Interview – Peter Beresford

Positive circle of connection

I spoke to Peter Beresford about his life and work in public participation as a service user, campaigner, researcher and teacher, particularly in the fields of mental health and disability. His work has been characterised by a commitment to 'bottom-up' rather than 'top-down' forms of research and knowledge-sharing.

His early work with his partner, Suzy Croft, in the 1970s involved door-to-door participation with residents in south London to shape local planning and services. They found that most people felt disconnected from decisions in their neighbourhood. The results of their work were shared with local people in various ways, from shopfront displays and media coverage to household drops of accessible summaries. Involving people in research included a commitment to feed back the results and support further action.

Like others I have talked to, Peter talked about the need to humanise research. As he put it, 'we should bring all of ourselves and see all of other people in the work we do'. Often, academic language is distanced and alienating and researchers are disciplined to speak in a detached 'third person' way, devoid of context. But as humans, we want to relate to each other and connect.

Peter underlined the need for responsibility in research, given the potential to do harm as in past examples of research and practice in areas like overuse of medication in mental health policy. Researchers can feel powerless, particularly early in their career, in relation to funders, publishers or managers. Peter emphasised how researchers should own their power to do harm as well as good, linking academic activity to broader causes of social justice, social change and progress, as the 'emancipatory disability research' movement has sought to.

There are no shortcuts to meaningful and inclusive participation. Peter emphasised the challenges for researchers in finding the right people and working with them in the right way. But there are organisations and networks which can support good and diverse involvement, including the 'user led organisation' he helped to found Shaping Our Lives as an independent national network of disabled people and service users (www. shapingourlives.org.uk).). And the more effort in involving service users throughout any research project, the greater the chances that the research will be used and useful. Researchers should aim, in Peter's words, to create 'a positive circle of connection' with the communities they want to reach.

Step four: partner with organisations, networks and champions

A starting point for good communication is to understand your audience, who they trust and where they go to for information. Patient bodies, charities, advocacy organisations, resident groups and third sector organisations are often important as a collective voice for particular communities. These may be formal organisations with staff and foundations or self-organising networks for people with particular conditions or needs. Working with them you are likely to have better reach and are more likely to get your items on their newsletters, websites and mailouts. They may also help you to identify individuals with influence on social media, who are a trusted voice for the communities you are trying to reach.

Chapter 8 will look in more detail at the role of the media in presenting, promoting and only sometimes distorting research findings. Using print and broadcast media, as well as social media channels, can be a good way of amplifying your research. For instance, researchers in Southampton working on respiratory diseases were able to engage a broadsheet journalist in a sustained and evidence-informed campaign on air quality and health (see Box 8.2).

But often 'narrowcast' can be more effective than 'broadcast'. This means working with partner organisations to use their networks and established communities to engage in dialogue about research. At our evidence centre, we collected together research on pressing problems and in each case worked closely with patient or public members. This included disability and age-related charities and voluntary community groups on our report on assistive technology for older people. For our review of research on the organisation of stroke services, we worked with the Stroke Association. Through their networks, we engaged stroke survivors and carers in the shaping of the report and in the promotion of it through face-to-face events and activities of their regional and local branches. Input from stroke survivors and family carers on our steering group helped to give greater emphasis to the research on early supported discharge and rehabilitation programmes and the reality – and struggles – of life after hospital. Earlier drafts of our report had given more prominence to the acute phases of stroke management and care. People with lived experience also foregrounded research on particular rehabilitation activities – such as evidence on walking programmes – as positive contributions to the research story. They contributed patient vignettes to bring to life some of the research themes (Figure 5.4).

Figure 5.4: Patient experiences vignettes to illustrate research

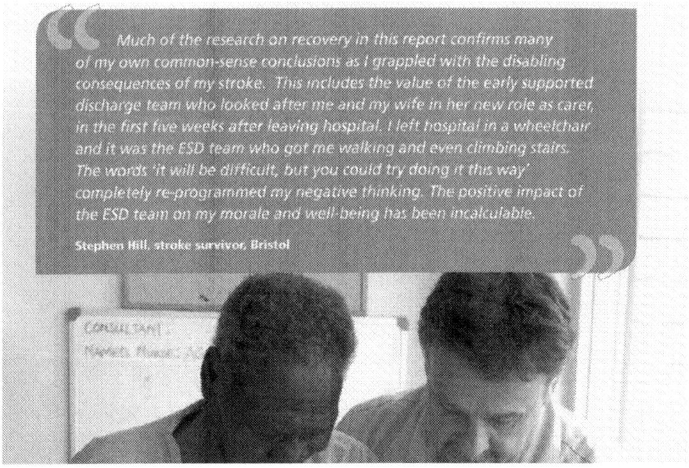

> Much of the research on recovery in this report confirms many of my own common-sense conclusions as I grappled with the disabling consequences of my stroke. This includes the value of the early supported discharge team who looked after me and my wife in her new role as carer, in the first five weeks after leaving hospital. I left hospital in a wheelchair and it was the ESD team who got me walking and even climbing stairs. The words 'it will be difficult, but you could try doing it this way' completely re-programmed my negative thinking. The positive impact of the ESD team on my morale and well-being has been incalculable.
>
> Stephen Hill, stroke survivor, Bristol

Source: NIHR (2017) Roads to recovery: organisation and quality of stroke services. doi: 10.3310/themedreview-001685

National organisations like Age UK or Mencap have skilled and effective communication teams, who are good at conveying complex research simply. They are also on the lookout for relevant research which will make good stories for their newsletters, campaigns and fundraising activities. Organisations and individuals can also advise on appropriate use of language, such as 'a person with diabetes' rather than 'a diabetic'. Working with advocacy groups, we changed our language in our learning disability services report from 'people with challenging behaviour' to 'behaviour which challenges'. These subtle differences are important.

Step five: present content which is engaging and accessible

Plain language summaries

A good test for any research is that you could explain your findings to another parent at the school gates or a fellow passenger on a bus. Many research funders now require plain language summaries of 300–500 words. We will consider in more detail in Chapter 9 how this is done and why it needs real investment of time and effort to get right. It is difficult to write clearly and simply about complex findings and stay true to the science. This includes giving some sense of the weight of evidence or level of certainty from your study in relation to the wider evidence. You also need to involve your target readers in the writing and editing of the summary.

There has been some knowledge translation type work to test, develop and refine these summaries working with panels of patients and general public (for instance, Synnot et al 2018). There is also a body of literature on parallel attempts to translate clinical guidelines for general and public use. One interesting example used content analysis for detailed review of patient versions of clinical practice guidelines and contrasted this with what the literature said patients and public wanted (Santesso et al 2016). They found that most guidelines for patients focused on disease, tests and treatment but had little information on issues of interest to patients such as benefits and harms, how to navigate the system or self-care advice. Few paid attention to beliefs, values and preferences. And not many patient versions used stories or scenarios to personalise the information for the reader. None of this is surprising. It is very difficult to make information simple, accurate and relevant to different contexts and readers. But it underlines the importance of public-facing summaries and setting aside time and resources to work with others to get it right.

Easy-read versions

In our review of research on learning disability services, we commissioned an advocacy group for people with learning disability (My Life My Choice) to work with us on an easy-read version of the report (Figure 5.5). Easy-read information is designed to be understood by people with learning disabilities, memory or language problems. Since 2016, those providing NHS and adult care services have to provide essential information in accessible formats for all users. Easy-read versions usually have

Figure 5.5: Easy-read version of research on learning disability services

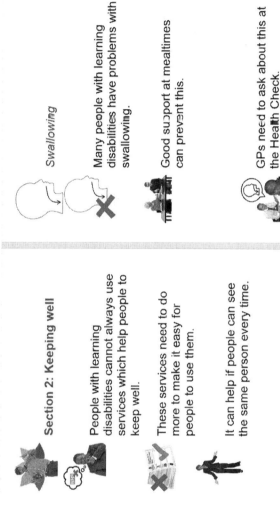

Section 2: Keeping well

People with learning disabilities cannot always use services which help people to keep well.

These services need to do more to make it easy for people to use them.

It can help if people can see the same person every time.

Swallowing

Many people with learning disabilities have problems with swallowing.

Good support at mealtimes can prevent this.

GPs need to ask about this at the Health Check.

Source: NIHR (2020) Better Health and Care for All – Easy Read. doi: 10.3310/themedreview-04328

much less text, use simple words and have photographs or images accompanying text. We had been engaging with the advocacy group from the start of the project and they produced the first draft of an easy-read version, using skilled facilitation to create and review text with people with learning disabilities. Our editorial team then went through several versions of the text to make sure the main messages stayed reasonably true to the science while being as clear as possible. This was quite difficult where there were mixed findings or a variety of study designs with varying levels of certainty and quality. For instance, our review featured four large evaluations of a complex person-centred approach for managing behaviour which challenged in residential settings. The findings were mixed and it was very difficult to find a way of conveying this which was clear but accurate. This was the first time I had engaged with easy-read format and I found it challenging to extract simple messages, but keep the nuance of the findings. Interestingly, although we had designed the easy-read report for people with learning disabilities and carers, many staff in NHS and residential care settings said it was their go-to version of the report. It is a good discipline for us all – can you make an easy-read version of your main report?

Choosing the right images

In our work packaging up evidence, we also learned the importance of images. Again, patient and user groups can be a great source of appropriate images, as many have picture libraries and resources. We were advised for instance not to use stock images to illustrate our review of evidence on services for people with serious mental illness. Too often these featured brooding or despairing shots of people with their head in their hands. Similarly, it was hard to find pictures of overweight people happily engaged in physical activity. The typically negative or bland visuals around older people sparked a viral campaign under the hashtag #nomorewrinklyhands. It is also important to reflect the diversity of populations and people who might be affected by your research.

PRACTICAL POINTERS ON REACHING PATIENTS, PUBLIC AND SERVICE USERS

Involve the right people throughout the study

When people are engaged in meaningful ways from early stages, it makes your job easier in promoting findings at the end. For instance, if some public members on your study team have written patient information leaflets or been involved in recruiting service users to take part in the research, they will have had to explain very simply and compellingly what your study is about and why it matters. Those involved in the study can act as ambassadors and help you understand which aspects are most interesting to people and why.

This step also involves thinking about which communities and individuals might be missing. What efforts do you need to take to capture different voices in your study, beyond the usual suspects? Have you tested out emerging findings with groups of patients or service users or advocacy groups working with you during the project? When sharing your findings, who do you want to reach and where do they go? Are there particular channels or media favoured by different groups or communities?

Write a summary for the general public

Researchers often spend far too little time on plain language summaries and public-facing versions of their work. This takes time to do well and should be done with the people who are the intended audience. Expect many iterations, testing it out with different people. It is a good test to read this out loud to check that it is as clear and simple as it can be (but no simpler). Use an online language test to review your summary against a standard. You should aim for it to be understood by an average 13-year-old.

Take it one step further and try to make it accessible for those with memory problems or learning disabilities or whose first language is not English. Creating a proper easy-read version of your work is a particular skill and may need specialist input, but it is a good test to try to explain your work to those who may find it a bit harder. There are guides to help with this, but the main take-home message is that public-facing summaries are important, but take time, skill and close working with others to do well.

Consider new ways of communicating to general audiences

Not everyone can produce a graphic novel or film based on their research findings. But it is worth taking time to consider how you could visualise the key 'storyline' of your work. This might take the form of infographics, service user vignettes or cartoons. A good way to communicate your findings is to have a conversation with a community group leader or patient advocate, perhaps through a podcast or video chat. You could also approach festivals and science fairs – which have included end of life researchers and clinicians sparking big conversations on where and how people die and how to make it better. There are people who can help you to do this well. This includes communications teams of target charities who can work with you to hone your messages in a short article which could reach patient and public audiences.

6

WHO you want to reach – policymakers and managers

Summary

This chapter sets out a few examples of high-impact research which has changed and influenced policy as well as practice. I then look at the theoretical and empirical research which tells us how policymakers make decisions and use evidence in the real world. Researchers need to understand this context and the messy and dispersed nature of policymaking, in a world of competing demands. Policymakers may rely on their instincts when responding to and acting on research. They also depend on trusted individuals and organisations, like thinktanks, to make sense of evidence. Researchers need to understand these chains of influence in their field. I interview the head of a What Works Centre and share learning on effective mechanisms of evidence use. As policymaking is so diffuse, it is worth looking at managers and health and social care system leaders as well as central government. I consider recent studies on how managers use evidence which confirms the central notion that 'evidence does not speak for itself'. The chapter concludes with research on packaging evidence for policymakers, with practical tips for writing effective policy briefs which may make your research more likely to be used by key decision-makers.

Who makes the decisions?

As well as the public, patients and staff, research can also make a difference to policy decisions and practice. This does not only mean understanding central policymakers in Westminster, Whitehall or Cardiff. In this chapter, when talking about policymakers, I mean those making decisions at a system or organisational (rather than team) level. This includes system leaders and managers. In health and social care, decision-making happens at all levels in a diffuse way. Your research might be useful to local directors of adult social care services, care home group chains, local commissioners, charity heads or hospital chief executives as well as civil servants and ministers. This chapter looks at what we know already from evidence on how policymakers access and use research and strategies to maximise uptake of findings. Although work in this area emphasises the complexity of policy systems and decision-making, researchers should not lose heart. There are many practical steps that researchers can take, working in partnership with others, to give your findings a better chance of influencing policy and shaping services.

Step one: ask the right questions

Let me start with a couple of examples of research which has influenced policy in different ways. These feature high-impact studies on widening access to talking therapies (Box 6.1) and research on nurse staffing levels (Box 6.2).

Box 6.1: Research example – talking therapies

It's good to talk

David Clark, a clinical psychologist at Oxford University, is one of the founders of the successful national programme to widen access for talking therapies. Despite clinical guidelines confirming the effectiveness of psychological therapies as the first choice for treating anxiety and depression, few patients were receiving best care. Many were waiting for more than 18 months to be seen. Since the formal launch of the programme to access these therapies in 2008, more than 10,500 therapists have been trained to deliver psychological therapies. Every year, more than a million people are now being treated, being seen on average within five weeks.

Success like this with hindsight looks inevitable. But even with strong research at its core, this was by no means a given and took many years. Hearing David Clark speak, it is clear that his clinical advocacy, persistence, connections and direct lobbying helped to achieve his ambitious goal of a nationally funded programme with a new workforce to deliver effective care. Some interesting features emerge from his story.

One was the force of serendipity – and networks – which helped to pair him with a labour economist, Richard Layard, after chatting in a coffee queue at a conference. The clinician and economist together wrote articles on the economic case for expanding access to proven psychological therapies. Their argument was compelling in terms of reduced suffering but also increased wellbeing and productivity at relatively modest cost (Layard et al, 2007). This also led to a public-facing book (*Thrive*) and an easy-read version produced with the charity MIND (*We Need to Talk*).

As well as getting broad public and targeted stakeholder support, Clark also employed direct lobbying tactics. He and Layard sent a memo to Prime Minister Tony Blair's Policy Unit in the run-up to the 2005 General Election. They were then invited to give a seminar to the Cabinet Office in January 2005. They distilled their message into some 'killer messages', including an estimate of the current problem in terms of reduced GDP of 4 per cent in untreated anxiety and depression. They made the case, and in May 2005 the programme to improve access to talking therapies was in the manifesto. Another feature of this successful campaign was to monitor and measure. The newly elected government supported demonstration sites in Doncaster and Newham, and evaluations of the pilots confirmed economic and clinical benefits, as predicted (Clark 2018). The full national programme was launched in 2008 and has since inspired similar models in Canada, Australia and Norway among other countries.

Of course not every researcher can land a direct briefing at Number 10. But the combination of having the right information – not just critical data on effectiveness and impact, but a range of tailored briefings – at the right time to influence policy action including manifesto pledges was crucial.

Box 6.2: Research example – safer staffing

What difference do nurses make?

Another example where research has influenced policy as well as practice is around workforce research. In the last 20 years, there has been high-quality research linking nurse staffing levels to hospital death rates, from the work of Linda Aiken in the US to more recent multi-country European cross-sectional RN4Cast study in Europe (Aiken et al 2014). While such research could not prove causal links, the high-quality cross-sectional study provided good evidence of associations between staffing and outcome. However, when, in the wake of concerns about failings relating to under-staffing at Mid Staffordshire, NICE commissioned two reviews of evidence to inform national guidance on safe staffing levels, this proved difficult.

The evidence base was advanced by recent work by Peter Griffiths and Jane Ball in Southampton (Griffiths et al 2018). Their NIHR study, part of a wider programme of work, showed that higher levels of registered nurses were associated with fewer missed observations (or 'care left undone'), reduced length of stay and adverse events, including mortality. The authors sought to address some of the limitations in the evidence base to date by linking data at the patient level and modelling the economic impact of changes in ward staffing. In this way, they were able to test possible causal mechanisms. Results showed that the relative risk of death increased by 3 per cent for every day registered nurse staffing fell below the ward average. As well as these key headline findings, there were interesting analyses about the relationship between registered nurses and support staff. This suggests that healthcare assistants are unlikely to make up for the shortfall of qualified nurses in terms of patient outcomes.

Box 6.3: Interview – Peter Griffiths

Can research answer policy questions?

Although the evidence on nurse staffing and patient outcomes is as good as it is likely to get, Peter Griffiths, Professor of Health Services Research at Southampton University (who styles himself as a 'workforce epidemiologist'), says there will always be a gap between what evidence can be reasonably provided and the questions which policymakers want addressed.

Talking to him, he says, 'We have a body of evidence that is being used to answer the question "how many nurses do we need?". The answer from the research so far has come back with the answer "more". But we do not know how much. More research might help us to better quantify the effects of investing in nursing staff and identify points at which there are diminishing returns, but decisions about what is "optimal" can never just be a matter of evidence. Defining an optimal staffing level depends on values – what level of quality we want, what outcomes we value most and what we are willing (and able) to pay for as a society as a whole.'

What can we take from this? We may be looking in the wrong place if we expect research to deliver a magic number, uncontested, which can address what is essentially a political and policy decision around priorities, constraints and levels of spend. However, high-quality evidence can go some way to setting the parameters for that decision and debate.

These examples show different ways in which research may create ripples of influence, sometimes over many years. Not all research has immediate traction with policy and policymakers. It is not always possible to set out a direct and track-able journey from research to decision. We know that it is often difficult or inappropriate to attribute effect to single studies – indeed, that is largely not how science or knowledge works. The slow drip of accumulating knowledge and meandering ways in which research may or may not reach places and people of influence may be hard to measure. Short-term impacts and instrumental effects are easier to track than research which changes the conversation.

Step two: understand the context

It is worth taking a step back to consider what we know about the context of policymaking in which evidence gets used. We can draw on the work of scholars like Paul Cairney[1] (Box 6.4) who uses theory and evidence in the fields of political science and policy studies to illuminate how research is used by decision-makers. Annette Boaz and Kathryn Oliver have also provided many insights into the interface between evidence and policy, drawing on many disciplines and fields (Oliver and Boaz 2019).

Box 6.4: Interview – Paul Cairney

Real-world policy and evidence use

I spoke to Paul Cairney, Professor of Politics and Public Policy at the University of Stirling, about his work on the relationship between research evidence and policy.

'The starting point for many researchers is that they want to know why policymakers "ignore" the evidence. Why is there this gap between good evidence and policy decisions?

There is a whole body of theory and research from political studies over some years which helps us answer that question.

First, think again about the question. Framing the problem as a gap between the research you produce and what happens to it is not helpful. Instead, find out how the policy process works and how your research might fit with this.

Second, understand the limited capacity of policymakers to pay attention. They have to have a very strong reason to read your research given the volume of information moving across their desk, so you need to articulate what is special and helpful about your work.

Third, policymaking is complex and distributed. People often think of a small group of people in charge making rational, considered decisions. In practice, it is messy and episodic, with important discussions happening with networks and people outside the room. You need to understand and work with these chains of influence.'

How policymakers use evidence

It is worth elaborating on some of these points, as they are critical to our understanding of how research has influence and impact on policymaking.

Rather like the shift of thinking on knowledge mobilisation, policy process is no longer seen as a simple linear model of stages from agenda setting to option appraisal and implementation (Cairney 2020). Instead, the reality is more dispersed, distributed and messier than 'policymaking-as-imagined'. Drawing on an established body of research on policymakers, Cairney notes:

> The political process encourages them to make decisions more quickly, in the face of uncertainty, while their attention tends to lurch, rather unpredictably, from issue to issue. Consequently, their demand for information may be unpredictable, and their ability to devote sufficient time, to understand the evidence, is very limited. Crucially, they *still make decisions*. (Cairney 2016: 16; emphasis in original)

Another point which is important for researchers understanding the mindset of policymakers is that 'they must find efficient ways to ignore almost all information, to make timely choices' (Cairney 2020). Given the size and scope of the state and decisions to be made, their aim is to reduce ambiguity – hence, the power of the nuggets of 'evidence' in the earlier example from Clark and Layard on the case for psychological therapies.

This information overload means that only clear, compelling messages achieve cut-through. And this works best when using emotional or belief-driven shortcuts, often relating to the power of storytelling (for a great discussion of the role of emotion in policymaking, see Drew Westen's book *The Political Brain*) (Westen 2008). Policymakers, from cabinet ministers to civil servants, are people who will have visceral responses to research which is relevant to them, perhaps their frail mother recovering from hip surgery or risks to their teenage children from online grooming.

It is not just how decisions are made but who makes the decisions that is different from what might be imagined. Rather than an individual or committee weighing formal evidence in a deliberative way at a particular moment, much decision-making happens over time in dispersed and distributed systems of influence. Ministers or other top decision-makers rely on civil servants or supporting staff who will themselves have networks with advocacy groups and trusted advisers. Again, rather than a visible cycle of decision-making at the top, the reality is that most activity happens in policy communities out of sight.

What can researchers do about this? Other parts of this chapter will look at involving the right people and the relational work in building or connecting with coalitions of interest; the role of intermediary bodies in the wider system, like What Works centres; and how to shape your research into tailored formats for policymakers like policy briefs. First, it is worth looking at local level decision-makers in the health system and how they use research.

How healthcare managers use evidence

Many of the lessons from Cairney's work on public policymaking resonate with a cohort of NIHR-funded observational studies on how service leaders in healthcare use evidence. For instance, Nicolini's ethnographic study shadowed hospital chief executives and characterised their information use as 'effective scanning activities' (Nicolini et al 2014). They rarely used discrete bits of knowledge or actively searched for formal research findings – instead, they delegated this to their top team or trusted staff (this study also showed how small the 'inner conversational circle' was – a feature often seen in central government as well). Their job was not to access research themselves but to 'join the dots' and make sense of a range of evidence from disparate sources.

We can see in these studies that we come back to many earlier themes of this book. What 'counts' as evidence is itself contested. Formal research has to compete with other, often more powerful forms of research. One study (Rushmer et al 2015) on evidence used by commissioners to develop and implement alcohol policies found that evidence on alcohol-related harms was augmented, interpreted and sometimes overtaken by local data and knowledge on context, geography, what had been tried before and local fit. Research by Dopson et al (2013) showed that formal research findings were least valued as a source of information for health managers. This was confirmed in observational work by Wye et al which noted:

> Media such as conversations and stories fitted particularly well with the fast-changing, flexible world of commissioning, and often 'trumped' hard data that could be questioned or sidelined on account of their low perceived usability. Local data often were more persuasive than national or research-based information. (Wye et al 2015: 131)

This illustrates that it is not just the 'what' but the 'who' and the 'how'. Looking at the empirical evidence on managers use of research, it is clear in the words of many that, 'Research does not speak for itself'. Managers often relied on others, such as medical directors or clinical advisers, to interpret and make sense of research, combining it with local data and experience on what worked recently. Indeed, Swan notes that often it required people with authority to *advocate* for the evidence and how it related to the problem in hand – 'Bringing the "evidence" to the table without the expert is almost always inadequate' (Swan et al 2012: 180). The importance of trusted advisers with personal influence to make the case for certain pieces of research is a theme which recurs in the literature.

Another aspect of 'what' (with an element of 'how') is the importance of data on costs and impact, seen in the example on psychological therapies. A review by Wallace et al on barriers and facilitators to use of systematic reviews by decision-makers showed the need for information on local applicability and costs and contextualisation of findings (Wallace et al 2012). What would it cost to implement here? How many emergency admissions could we avoid or how many months could older people in our district stay living independently in their own homes? We will look in more detail later in this chapter at the format for packaging research in ways which are more likely to appeal to policymakers and managers.

Step three: involve the right people

As we discovered earlier, policymakers and managers are unlikely to turn to academic journals direct for evidence. Instead, they rely on intermediary bodies, like thinktanks, and trusted advisers and colleagues who have already digested and interpreted research to meet the policy need. Jo Maybin carried out ethnographic work in English health departments, looking at how policymakers made decisions (Maybin 2016). She concluded that there was reliance on personal networks, colleagues seen to have knowledge and contacts or 'contacts of contacts' with influence from professional bodies, charities, thinktanks and advocacy groups. Policymakers were more likely to seek personal contact – what she calls 'embodied knowledge' – wanting judgement, as well as 'facts' from trusted sources. The risk of loss of organisational memory when colleagues or external contacts moved on makes this a tricky strategy, but it is very hard-wired into ways of working for senior policymakers. The same was true in Nicolini's study of chief executives of NHS organisations and their over-reliance on a small cabal of trusted advisers and colleagues (Nicolini et al 2014). Researchers with something to say need to find ways to influence policy and decision-making when it happens and where it happens.

Since personal contacts with policymakers are difficult to forge and maintain, researchers working on a topic need to form effective coalitions with other interested parties, from professional bodies to patient groups. Working with others provides reassurance to decision-makers of a concerted focus or 'single voice' and enable a wider set of influencers to make the most of opportunities which arise. This is essential given the time it takes for evidence to influence policy and the diffuse nature of policymaking, as shown in Cairney's case study of tobacco control with decades-long efforts by scientists and health groups to get recognition of the problem as a public health priority and support for evidence-based policy solutions (Cairney 2016).

Step four: partner with organisations, networks and champions

Many policymakers in health and social care rely for evidence on intermediary bodies such as thinktanks, charities and research institutes. In the UK, there is also the What Works Network, a set of bodies aiming to put evidence at the heart of public policy and decision-making. This is explicit in their remit – 'to improve the way government and other organisations create, share and use (or "generate, transmit and adopt") high quality evidence for decision-making'.[2] These focus on a range of public services and arenas, from criminal justice and economic generation to education and wellbeing. The inspiration for these bodies was the setting up of NICE in 1999 with a focus on evidence-based treatments and mechanisms for making decisions about high-cost new technologies. A good account of these bodies is given by Jonathan Breckon and David Gough, including the ways in which their activities have been contested and perceived as exercises in managerial control of research (Breckon and Gough 2019). I interviewed the head of one What Works Centre (Box 6.5) who gave me interesting insights into how evidence does and doesn't influence policy.

Box 6.5: Interview – Nancy Hey

Finding opportunities for influence

The What Works Wellbeing Centre was set up in 2014 with a focus on wellbeing and what government, business, communities and individuals can do to improve it. Nancy Hey was the founding director of this Centre and spoke to me about her experience in getting research to decision-makers.

'From my time working across government, I know that officials want to use evidence but they're going to make decisions regardless, events move fast, so the best thing you can do is to get as much evidence into their thinking as possible.'

Follow the science – mechanisms and behaviour

'When we set up our What Works Centre, we did a review on what works for research use (see Figure 6.1). We found six mechanisms. We over-weight our efforts on mechanisms like getting policymakers and researchers together in a room by holding a roundtable or reception for MPs. Events like these are very popular, very resource-intensive and yet there is very little evidence to show that it makes much difference. Unlike other mechanisms, where we really know they are important, like good communication and building research into decision-making systems – like system flags for clinicians to ask about smoking, which don't rely on individuals being hugely enthusiastic themselves. And this is where our knowledge of mechanisms needs to relate to what we know of behavioural insights – we tend to over-estimate peoples' motivation as a driver.'

Make it easy

'Busy people don't want to click on lots of different headings and levels to find out what something's about. Make it as easy as possible to get to the parts that matter. When I brief a government minister on a complex topic like say community resilience, you have a couple of sides maximum, but they won't read all of it. Start with the findings. And try to be as clear as possible. There is good advice from government on web design and creating accessible documents www.gov.uk/guidance/publishing-accessible-documents.'

Engaging audiences

'Strategic communication is important – engaging stakeholders and segmenting our audience. Each strand has many dimensions to it, for instance government includes national, devolved, local and elected members, officials and analysts in public sector. The more specific you can be the better in addressing your particular audience. And knowing their channels – for instance, a piece from us on wellbeing at work or corporate responsibility in Business Insider will reach places our website won't.

> It's too late at the end of your project to try to get important policymakers involved. If the right people are involved in some way early on, there is a pull for the evidence which follows – your audience is ready.'

Communication, dissemination and engagement activities at the What Works Centre for Wellbeing are prioritised in a strategic way, drawing on a useful review of evidence on approaches to getting research to decision-makers (Langer et al 2016). As well as formal evidence from 25 published reviews – skewed towards health, the source of most evidence to date on evidence-based policy and practice – there is a useful broader overview of learning from other fields in social sciences, like behavioural science, social marketing and adult learning theory.

Looking at over 150 interventions in the formal review across these different kinds of evidence use mechanisms, sometimes used in combination, it was striking how little evidence of impact there was in certain fields. There was reasonable evidence to support good communication strategies and design, skills-building on evidence literacy and structural ways of embedding evidence (Figure 6.1). There was less evidence of impact for relationship-building exchanges between researchers and policymakers – although this may just reflect how difficult it is for these kinds of informal activities to be evaluated and measured in systematic ways. Overall, there were richer insights and learning from the broad scoping work in diverse fields of social sciences than the narrow effectiveness search in the formal literature review.

Strategies and tactics to optimise research uptake include, in Cairney's formulation, 'identifying where the action takes place; learning about the properties of subsystems, the rules of the game, and how to frame evidence to fit policy agendas; forming coalitions with other influential actors; and, engaging in the policy process long enough to exploit windows of opportunity' (Cairney 2016: 81). It also means understanding the limits of policymakers' attention and the need for short, targeted summaries which appeal to the frames and feelings of the reader.

Figure 6.1: Prioritising engagement activity according to the evidence – what works in research use

Mechanism	Evidence		Pathway	Activity	Priority
CHAMPION evidence-informed decision making	ⓐ	No/Low	Motivation Opportunity	Use in combination Approach: Be curious with rigour Case studies, partners, norms	Low
DEFINE good evidence with community	ⓐ	No/Low	Motivation Opportunity	Use in combination GRADE & SERQUAL, DELPHI, evidence journey, evaluation guidance, methods series	Medium (important for sector)
VISIBLE evidence through access and communications	ⓐⓑⓒ	Reliable	Motivation Opportunity combined	Synthesis, design, UX, index/tools, digital, comms channels, networks, A-I-A, Tail	High
INTERACTION between decision makers and researchers	ⓐⓑ	Cautious	Ineffective for capability Motivation Opportunity	Use in combination Approach: Be curious with rigour Case studies, partners, norms	Medium
LEARNING building evidence skills and make sense of evidence	ⓐⓑⓒ	Reliable	Motivation Opportunity	Use in combination Approach: Be curious with rigour Case studies, partners, norms	Medium (where resources available)
ADOPTION through decision-making structures and processes	ⓐⓑⓒ	Reliable	Motivation Opportunity	Use in combination Approach: Be curious with rigour Case studies, partners, norms	High

Source: **What Works Centre for Wellbeing** under the Creative Commons license 4.0, adapted from Langer et al 2016.

Step five: present content which is engaging and accessible

Writing a policy brief

There is a small but growing evidence base on what managers and policymakers *say* they value about formats of evidence. This is largely qualitative research where individuals or groups of managers are asked to identify features that they find engaging or off-putting in research and research summaries. Findings from this research are summarised in reviews (Oliver et al 2014; Wallace et al 2014; Tricco et al 2016), which include the following barriers (I have picked out the main items here):

- lack of relevant content;
- lack of contextualisation of findings;
- length of paper or report;
- poor presentation format;
- too much on methods or research quality.

In terms of what they liked in the way of format, this mirrored the list of aforementioned negatives, but with some positive suggestions by managers, including:

- one-page top summary;
- graded format with key messages upfront;
- use of white space and bullets;
- more on implications for policy;
- web-based format preferred;
- framing title as question.

Particularly important for decision-makers is the need for information with local applicability and costs (Wallace et al 2012). Others have noted the importance for decision-makers of research where the implementation, economy and equity impacts are explicitly considered (Vogel et al 2013). It is a good exercise to test out the relevance of your findings for decision-makers. This might mean extrapolating findings to the footprint of an integrated care system for service leaders – how could this change impact on number of emergency hospital admissions in our area? At a national level, it might mean projected outcomes using employment and criminal justice data if new approaches for care leaver support were adopted.

Wickremasinghe and colleagues (2016) carried out a literature search, including grey literature such as advice for civil servants, and expert interviews, to identify what forms of evidence synthesis policymakers want. An important finding was that policymakers often want answers to broad questions, while researchers need to frame tight and narrow research or review questions as part of a commitment to reliability and reproducibility. But there is good agreement on the importance of readability, relevance and rigour – noting the tensions and trade-offs between rigour and relevance, if policy windows (see Chapter 7 on timing) are too short for a complete and systematic review of evidence on a given topic (Thomson 2013).

One important aspect is to start with the problem facing the decision-maker and not your study. This means knowing which topics have high policy salience and providing enough context to your research to underline their relevance and importance to topical issues of the day (Moat et al 2013). Keeping up to date with health and social care policy through service and practice journals, thinktank briefings and conferences is helpful. Framing your study according to policy need is the difference between 'pull' where the decision-maker wants the information and 'push' where you as a researcher are promoting your study. At our evidence centre, we pulled together relevant evidence starting with the problems facing policymakers, from safe levels of nurse staffing to improving care and outcomes for people with learning disabilities.

Box 6.6: Briefings for politicians

The Parliamentary Office for Science and Technology was set up 30 years ago to provide reliable evidence for the UK parliament. It provides helpful tips on how to prepare policy-facing briefs: https://post.parliament.uk/how-to-write-a-policy-briefing/. While much of this is familiar advice on good writing, there are some particular tips for evidence focused at parliamentarians, such as connecting the topic to data – numbers and stories – for particular areas and regions to get the attention of MPs. There is a library of structured short briefings for government on a range of topics, from cloud computing to marine renewables: https://post. parliament.uk/type/postnote/.

The policy brief championed by John Lavis et al (2009) and others is a way of focusing first on the pressing policy problem. Their series describing and supporting tools for increasing the uptake of trials and systematic reviews by decision-makers were a landmark in the health-related evidence-informed policy debate. They pioneered a format of briefing for decision-makers, including those in low- and middle-income countries.

To get a sense of the format of policy briefs, it is a good idea to browse existing resources (Box 6.6). Some of the key format and content principles useful for getting – and keeping – the attention of decision-makers include:

Start with the findings upfront

Begin with a declarative title or paragraph in which you explain your key findings and what they mean.

Explain why it is important

Set the findings in the context of policy and why this is important now. Identify uncertainties in current decision-making and how this research will fill some of these gaps. Link to recent events or crises which underline why new policy is needed.

Keep methods to a minimum

Say enough about study design for the reader to understand the weight of evidence. Put some critical information in sidebars or boxes, so you don't detract from the main messages.

Implications, not recommendations

State what the implications for policy might be from your research, but don't stray too far into explicit policy recommendations as you may be out of your depth (Whitty 2015). This might include consideration of costs and sustainability of initiatives, if scaled up.

The last word should come from Katherine Oliver and Paul Cairney (2019), who carefully reviewed formal research and grey literature across different disciplines to come to the following practical advice for researchers in reaching policymakers (Box 6.7).

Box 6.7: Tips for researchers to influence policy

- do high quality research;
- make your research relevant and readable;
- understand policy processes;
- be accessible to policymakers: engage routinely, flexible, and humbly;
- decide if you want to be an issue advocate or honest broker;
- build relationships (and ground rules) with policymakers;
- be 'entrepreneurial' or find someone who is;
- reflect continuously: should you engage, do you want to, and is it working?

Source: Oliver, K. and Cairney, P. (2019)

This paper is well worth reading in full, as an overview of existing guidance from a wide and dispersed evidence base (Oliver and Cairney 2019). As a critical review, it also helpfully highlights the tensions and unexamined contradictions in much 'how to' advice on influencing policymakers – for instance, whether researchers should present themselves as disinterested voices of science or as champions for particular causes. Both are legitimate, but require different activities and skillsets (and perhaps personalities).

There is a danger that the sum effect of this chapter is to make researchers feel disheartened about their ability to influence policy and decision-making. I am aware that research in this area emphasises the complexity (Lamont 2020) and diffuse nature of policymaking, which may lead to a counsel of despair. However, there are also examples of research throughout this book which have shaped policy, from understanding the weekend effect of hospital admissions to organisation of stroke services. Effective research teams I know use a range of approaches, hard and soft, to make their research land in policy circles.

PRACTICAL POINTERS TO REACH POLICYMAKERS AND MANAGERS

Understand chains of influence for your field of study

Map out who are the players in your field, some of whom you may have come across in your research already. Who are the influencers at foundations or lobby groups or thinktanks with a special interest in your field? Who do they work with? How does your work link into ongoing policy discussions and questions? As a researcher on self-funding residential places, you might want to dip into sessions of a parliamentary select committee inquiry on future funding of adult social care. As a radiographer you may want to find out more about central policy direction on imaging networks as a context and frame for your study.

Write a policy brief

Construct your findings as a one-page policy brief. Start with the headline findings upfront. Ground this in the context of the important policy problem it addresses, explaining what this adds to what we already know. Present implications of your research in terms of critical health or wellbeing benefits, costs, service efficiencies or equity impacts. Include important data points as boxed items. Use white space and consider the layout to emphasise the main take-home points. Test this brief out with policy leads or proxies.

Follow the debate

You can be a 'lurker' and perhaps participant in Twitter discussion. Identify people you admire in your field with a policy bent, read their posts and see who they follow, understand what the debates are and how they are framed. Identify relevant hashtags for events, campaigns or communities who may be interested in your work. Join in when you can, for instance signposting useful research articles at the right time in Twitter exchanges or Tweetchats. Attend relevant thinktank briefings, webinars, conferences – many of which are now free and online. Share a few insights from speakers which resonated with you and make links to relevant research. You can play your part in enriching policy debates with useful research.

7

WHEN you could have most impact

Summary

Perfect research which comes too late is no good for decision-makers. The importance of timing is often underestimated. The starting point is to try to ensure your research is relevant when it finishes and understand any important recent changes in policy or service landscape which may affect the way your results land. Some factors can be predicted, but researchers can also find 'hooks' that play research back into the issues of the day. Some examples are given of research which achieved topicality, including researchers studying the 'weekend effect' in hospitals and centralising stroke services. The use of interim findings and estimates of 'lives saved' at a critical point helped researchers to influence important decisions about stroke reconfiguration at the right time. Other examples on COVID-19 services show how researchers can be nimble in responding to rapidly changing contexts. Some international examples show how the readiness of the environment often trumps the quality of research in terms of impact.

It's all about timing

The health economist Martin Buxton once said that it is always too early to evaluate a health technology until, suddenly, it is too late (Drummond and Banta 2009). This is particularly true for complex health evaluations, like workforce or service models. They need to have had enough time to have bedded in and be stable enough to ensure that the approach could be adopted elsewhere and the way it works is understood. But waiting too long for an innovation to 'mature' may risk that an evaluation comes too late to change practice. New approaches, such as models of integrated care models, hospices at homes or virtual wards became widespread often in advance of formal evaluations. Landing your research findings at the right time can be critical to how many people it reaches and what difference it makes.

Thinking about the timing of research, it is useful to consider Kingdon's 'multiple streams analysis' (Kingdon 1995). He argues that a 'policy window' opens when three separate streams of problems, politics and policy come together. Each stream has its own flows, blocks and momentum. But for policy to change, there needs to be a well-defined narrative around the problem; a favourable political climate; and a workable solution or policy. These can sometimes be nudged forward by what Kingdon calls policy entrepreneurs, those agents with knowledge and influence in policy worlds. These may be professional leaders, thinktank analysts or lobbyists who are connected well with different advocacy networks.

Mintrom (2019) has described the attributes and strategies used by the policy entrepreneur to advance causes or campaigns. While researchers themselves will not usually fall into this category – although some examples are given in this book of academics who are 'energetic actors ... to promote policy innovations' (Mintrom 2019) – they may need to identify them. Finding out who are the movers and shakers in a particular field and working with them will help to identify the opportunities and windows for change.

What is the next hot topic?

In health research, much of the impact in timing outputs is down to the initial focus and relevance of the study. At the time of commissioning, the research funder and study team need to be confident that their findings will be meaningful and relevant in three to five years' time when the project is complete. NIHR uses deliberative processes with stakeholders to identify and prioritise research questions in relation to the agendas of management, delivery and use of services. Which are the most pressing questions? Will research findings from completed studies still be relevant in five years' time? Can we anticipate the problems and solutions on the horizon?

While the importance and urgency of research topics can be tested out with target audiences, it can be hard to predict the momentum of the political stream (in Kingdon's frame). For instance, NIHR had identified 24/7 working in the NHS as one of the top uncertainties where more research was needed in 2013. This was one of the priorities identified in a series of surveys, workshops and participative processes with patients, managers, clinical leaders and researchers. A call was put out to researchers and a number of projects were funded.

The issue of providing specialist cover and services across the week had been an important operational issue for the NHS for some time. But researchers in 2013 proposing careful analysis of routine hospital admission data could not have anticipated how the 'weekend effect' would become front-page news, linked to disputes between the government and junior doctors on medical contracts during 2016. Indeed, an early academic output (Meacock et al 2017) from the research team studying admissions and mortality across the week became the subject of cross-examination for the Health Minister and Chief Executive of NHS England at a Health Select Committee session.[1]

With hindsight, we can see that seven-day working ticks a number of boxes for rising high on the policy agenda. In policy analysis terms (Hogwood and Gunn 1984), this includes an issue which has reached crisis proportions; achieved particularity (that is, is focused and understandable); is emotive and engages human interest; has wide impact; and raises questions about power and legitimacy. In this case, all these factors came together at a particular political moment.

Catching the moment

Chapter 6 showed how we now understand more about the messy and dispersed nature of policymaking. There may not be a single policy 'window' – instead, there will be 'lurches of attention' by decision-makers. What this means for researchers is being nimble, flexible and paying attention to debates and moments as they unfold. As Cairney and Kwiatkowski note (2017), 'Their [researchers'] effectiveness comes from an investment of resources to generate knowledge of the political system and its "rules of the game", build up trust in the information they provide, and form coalitions, all of which helps them know when to act decisively when the time is right' (Cairney and Kwiatkowski 2017).

A good example of this was the NIHR study evaluating the impact of centralising stroke services in London and Manchester, led by Naomi Fulop (Box 7.1). The team was able to work with service networks and release findings at a time to influence planning decisions on the scale of future change. This example shows the impact of early and sustained engagement with clinical and service stakeholders as well as stroke charities and patient groups throughout the study. Promotion activity included a series of imaginative and participative seminars with service leaders, working with an innovative events company.

Box 7.1: Research example – stroke configuration

Saving lives in Manchester

In 2014, Greater Manchester had been aiming to centralise services further for some time, but change had been delayed. In London, where radical centralisation took place so that all patients were seen in hyperacute stroke units, the mixed-methods evaluation found reductions in mortality and length of stay above and beyond reductions observed elsewhere. In Greater Manchester, where only a selection of patients were seen in hyperacute units, there were no reductions in patient deaths beyond what was observed elsewhere (but shorter hospital stays). Qualitative research published later as part of this study showed how implementation models differed, with simpler, more inclusive referral pathways and a 'big bang' launch of changes in London, supported by quality standards (linked with financial incentives) and hands-on facilitation, compared to a more complex and phased approach in Manchester (Fulop et al 2019).

Sharing early findings with clinical leaders, engaged throughout the study, influenced decisions in Manchester to push forward a more complete centralisation of services. Before the results were published in the BMJ (Morris et al 2014) and having discussed with the stroke network, health economist Steve Morris produced an estimate that an additional 50 deaths per year could potentially be prevented by this further reorganisation. Local leaders harnessed this figure to argue against any further delays to implementation.

This figure was central to the publicity campaign, which supported local buy-in for the new system from the public, local authorities, commissioners, and providers in GM. This included an infographic produced by the local network, a briefing and tweets from local provider and commissioner organisations (under the hashtag #gmstroke). Greater Manchester agreed and implemented a fully centralised model in 2015.

Latest published findings by the team show the sustained impact of these changes (Morris et al 2019). In 2015, more than four out of five stroke patients in Manchester were treated in a hyperacute unit, more than double the rate with partial changes five years earlier. The researchers estimated that there were around 69 fewer deaths a year in Manchester, and recent national stroke audit data confirm that stroke services in this area remain among the highest performing in England.

Mobilising research at a time of crisis

More recently, we have seen research teams and the wider system rise to the new challenge of the COVID-19 pandemic. Research has been delivered at pace and findings have been quickly made available to meet urgent demands. This includes an evaluation of new ways of supporting people at home (Box 7.2).

Box 7.2: Research example – home oximetry monitoring

Keeping people with COVID-19 safe at home

Teams led by Naomi Fulop in London and Judith Smith in Birmingham carried out a three-month rapid evaluation of home monitoring or virtual wards during the pandemic between July and September 2020. These systems arose to monitor people with COVID-19 who may be getting worse at home, sometimes using pulse oximetry to check oxygen levels, to help them be admitted to hospital at the right time or stay safely at home. This was a new way of working for the service, with models set up in days or weeks rather than months. The team wanted to assess how well these had worked and what could be learned for future shocks or crises. This study consisted of a rapid review of evidence, brief data-collection exercise at eight sites to review staffing models, costs and patient experience and implementation study. From this work, the team established a typology of models which were either primary-led, secondary-led, step-down hospital care or mixed, with particular issues in each category. The implementation study showed how service leadership and collective goodwill supported very rapid change. Problems ranged from unclear referral criteria and pathways to availability of pulse oximeter devices and data challenges, particularly for primary care-led models. Findings from this project were shared with central policymakers in the UK, virtual ward collaboratives and newly formed communities like the NHS home pulse oximetry learning network.

Box 7.3: Interview – Naomi Fulop

Speed dating – build on good relationships with stakeholders

I talked to Naomi Fulop, Professor of Health Care Organisation and Management at UCL, who reflected on the rapid nature of this project on home oximetry monitoring during the pandemic. What would she say to other researchers?

'I have learned that it is possible to carry out work rapidly without compromising standards, when it really matters. It helps to have good relations in place with key stakeholders – you can build new relationships virtually, but that can be difficult. It's important to grab opportunities as they come. I worked closely with the national clinical advisor on sepsis and deterioration and colleagues, who helped me share findings with existing service networks. In one week, I was able to reach many hundreds of important local decision-makers across the country through sessions at different learning networks and communities of practice. That was partly possible because these events were virtual. But the main enabler was having the relationship with clinical and service influencers and real interest from staff in the work that we were doing.'

Sometimes researchers need to be flexible and respond to a changing context. The present COVID-19 epidemic shows many ways – some creative – in which researchers have accelerated or repurposed their work to serve decision-maker needs (Box 7.3).

Box 7.4: Research example – sharing emerging evidence on Long COVID

What do we know about Long COVID?

A group of clinicians, patients and researchers met in the summer of 2020 to consider evidence on the management and services for people living with COVID-19 and experiencing long-term effects. There was little published research at that time, but drawing on the lived experience of existing support groups and practitioners, some particular problems and research needs were identified. This included a growing recognition of the different constellations of fluctuating symptoms which made it difficult to diagnose and to access or plan appropriate services. Given the emergent state of evidence, a dynamic review was judged helpful which could signpost recently commissioned research relevant to those living with COVID-19 and resources from professional bodies and patient groups, as well as identifying questions for future research, recently updated with a second report (NIHR 2020). The report author, Elaine Maxwell, noted: 'We know a bit more every day about this phenomenon. There is a lot of research just starting, but it will not be ready for some time. Our aim in this report was to use the insights now from speaking to people living with COVID-19 to shape the services that are offered now and the research we need to improve support and care.' Parts of the review were updated in March 2021 as more evidence became available (NIHR 2021). The report signals the known unknowns and provides a roadmap for future research and service development.

The pandemic has accelerated our need for more dynamic models of research synthesis. But many developments to increase the responsiveness of evidence production and use were already underway. This includes living systematic reviews, defined by Elliott et al (2014) as reviews which are 'continually updated, incorporating relevant new evidence as it becomes available'. This recognises that updating can be intermittent, teams disbanding or taking too long in stop-start fashion to provide information which decision-makers need at the right time on topics of importance. Indeed, Shojania et al (2007) estimated that almost a quarter of reviews within two years of publication had not taken into account new evidence which would change understanding of the benefits or harms of treatments. Other developments, from use of big data and automated data-mining to crowdsourcing, are driving new expectations of the timelines for finding and synthesising evidence. While much of this debate has been around formal systematic reviews and controlled trials – with parallel debates on living clinical guidelines – this does not just apply to biomedical research. The call for greater efficiency and responsiveness can be seen in all kinds of health and care research.

When is when?

We talk about research having impact or being used, but it is often difficult to measure precisely. What counts as evidence being used? There is now a growing body of knowledge looking at adoption of research into practice with complex and overlapping time lags (see for instance, Hanney et al 2015), but there is still a common assumption of a fixed point where research has traction. Theoretical works like Carl May's influential normalisation process theory provide a structured way of studying how innovations take hold and become part of mainstream practice (May and Finch 2009). This has spawned a whole branch of theory-led implementation studies including, for example, a timely application of this approach to study the rapid transformation to remote working for office staff under COVID-19 (Carroll and Conboy 2020).

What interests me though is the dissonance between the assumed 'when' in many accounts of research promotion and use and the reality. Some time back, the researchers Hutchinson and Huberman (1994) looked at the spread of innovative practice in teaching science and mathematics in schools. They concluded that 'even when linear models for dissemination were "successful" in getting a product through the classroom door, they were not decisive in firmly rooting the innovation in place'. In order for that to happen, the findings had to resonate with what 'felt right' to teachers and school leaders and their lived experience.

In a very different context, DuVal and Shah (2020) looked at decisions about antiretroviral medication regimes by policymakers in different sub-Saharan African countries. Their fascinating analysis showed little congruence between the timing and publication of 'best' evidence of clinical effectiveness and uptake into policy and practice. The authors noted that 'gold-standard scientific evidence played a relatively minor role' in influencing policy. Much more important was a sense of momentum across the subcontinent towards a particular regimen, how easy it seemed to implement and how well it aligned with existing service models. Again, we can see the complex journey of evidence into decisions, making it difficult to predict and measure time taken to have traction.

In both these examples, the importance of context and 'readiness' of the environment is as (or more) important as the quality and relevance of the research itself. Factors include alignment with wider policy – 'what we need to do', professional wisdom or values – 'how we care for people' – and organisational culture – 'how we do things here'. These will all affect how and when research will land and make a difference. Although many aspects will be outside the control of individual researchers and research teams, there is much that can be done to maximise your chances to influence policy and practice.

PRACTICAL POINTERS TO WHEN YOU COULD HAVE MOST IMPACT

Know your context

You need to keep abreast of policy and service developments, which may make a difference to the context in which your research lands. That might mean browsing the *HSJ, Social Work* or *Caring Today*, or other target 'trade press' (see also, social media). Having practitioners and others on your project steering group will also help you to stay relevant and informed. This includes what is important now and scanning the horizon for future developments. Building and maintaining relationships with key service contacts will help you to be able to identify 'windows of opportunity' when your research might land.

Little and often

Have a plan for sharing interim and early findings in a responsible way. Research funders now encourage flexible ways of promoting research, as long as agreed quality checks are met. This may include preparing embargoed versions of your work and developing rapid preprint outputs. If there is a window of influence, you may want to consider slidepacks, toolkits and tailored outputs for particular audiences.

Reflect back

Think back on a past project. What do you know now about factors which affected the reception of these findings? What could you have done differently to increase relevance or impact? Could you have anticipated some of the changes in policy or practice at the outset? What sources of intelligence could have helped you pitch this better?

8

HOW to reach people – use of stories and the media

Summary

You need to understand how to tell the story of your research. This chapter sets out why narrative is important and explores in detail the mechanisms by which stories work. In health and care research, there is a risk that individual vignettes can distort rather than illuminate wider evidence bases. This is illustrated with some examples from patient safety. Tools from persuasion, advertising and marketing are described briefly. Social media can be used by researchers to engage wider audiences and to connect in different ways. Examples are given of use of Twitter and research projects using a range of media effectively. Interviews with leading journalists and communicators provide further insights in capturing the interest and attention of general readers.

Power of stories

An actor friend once told me of a time in his life when he was working in a regional theatre. They were visited routinely by the local fire department carrying out health and safety checks and each time were cautioned for blocking fire exits with stacks of flammable sets. The fire officer read out the regulations they were violating and the fines which could be incurred. The actors and theatre manager promised to move the sets and store them somewhere else but soon lapsed into old habits. The reproof became almost a ritual. One time, the fire officer changed tack. He brought with him real pictures of the charred and maimed bodies of children who had been trapped in a house fire. He told the assembled actors their names and ages and shared an earlier family photograph. He described arriving at the scene with the terrible heat, the cries of the parents, crackle and thump of the structure caving in and the smell of scorched wood and plastic, the sweat of fellow officers fighting the fire and knowing what they would find. My friend said that after that point, the exits were always kept clear.

Stories help us to understand others. Stories stay with us. Stories make us want to know more. In the case mentioned previously, it was a story that motivated action to keep people safe. Researchers can learn much from journalists, like Shaun Lintern (Box 8.1) on the art of telling stories well. This chapter has practical advice on using the media and what social media can offer the researcher wanting to reach wider audiences. But first we start with a look at the way in which stories get people's attention, for better or worse.

Box 8.1: Interview – Shaun Lintern

Read all about it

Shaun Lintern is health correspondent of *The Independent* and was named health journalist of the year in 2019 for his work uncovering failings in maternity care. He spent many years at the *Health Service Journal* raising the profile of quality and patient safety issues and helped to uncover the serious harms at Mid Staffordshire hospital early in his career as a local news reporter.

I was lucky to talk to him between deadlines in the middle of a pandemic, having started his job not long after the biggest health event of our lifetime erupted – 'suddenly I'm the most important person in the newsroom'. I talked to him about what researchers could do to reach wider audiences and he started with some frustrations. In his work as an investigative reporter, for instance looking into maternity services issues, he had struggled to access important papers on foetal monitoring or other aspects of safety. 'Many important research findings are hidden behind paywalls or downloaded in very low numbers but tell important stories that deserved wider airing. I have worked well with researchers, like Alison Leary on nurse staffing, where she released her findings under embargo, giving me time to prepare a story properly with the right facts and emphasis. This got a wider readership not just for my news piece but also linking back to her academic paper – those accessing it were people actually running clinical services and making the decisions about staffing. One mode enhances the other.

We need to bridge these two worlds of research and the press – I know that most researchers want to make things better, like journalists. I count my readers in the millions, most journals count them in dozens or hundreds. I get some material coming through on drugs, devices, technology but rarely get academics approaching me with work about how services are run. Researchers should think about working with journalists on embargo basis to communicate findings, discuss what they mean in the real world, build an actual news story based on the foundation of the research with context and case studies. We can work together on a story in the public interest. I need time to think creatively about how I can make it dance and sing as a news story.

As a mainstream journalist, I use individuals and stories to drive home the points. Data alone isn't enough to convince clinicians to change practice – you need those real-world stories. I came across this powerfully: a consultant wanting to improve sepsis care at his trust gave his colleagues performance data on sepsis care bundles – no real change. And then he tried a different route, confronting clinicians with real patients, going to Dr Smith and saying this patient Mrs Bloggs had poor outcomes and antibiotics not given in first hour and so on, and that's when the change came. The stories can't be the sole basis of an article; you need data and research as well. I always look in my journalism for systemic issues but I use an individual family to illustrate a wider issue. Once you've got the audience to engage with that one family and then you tell your reader they are just one of a hundred similar families, I think it carries much more weight. You've already got their attention.'

Why do stories matter?

Stories are the telling of events in a structured way. This is done by choosing what order to tell events and what to leave out or keep in, using narrative skills to keep audiences entertained and interested. There is now a well-established theory and science on the power of storytelling. Evolutionary biology, neuroscience and psychology all tell us how we humans are wired to enjoy stories and to share social information. As Brian Boyd and other scholars of narrative have noted, communities have always used stories to solve problems, alert each other to danger, share advice and make sense of the world together (Boyd 2009).

Some of my favourite non-fiction books have involved expert storytelling. This includes oral histories on the great depression by Studs Terkel 50 years ago (Terkel 1970). His skilful selection, editing and ordering of first-person accounts show us the complexity and richness of everyday lives, more compelling than a novel. Juxtaposing the reports of lean times for the broker, the seamstress, the linotype operator, the Pullman porter, the coalminer he gives voice to the extraordinary ordinary. Oliver Sacks invented a new genre popularising neuroscience with his compelling case stories. Who can forget the eponymous hero of the book on the man who mistook his wife for a hat, whose brain had stopped being able to understand what his eyes were seeing? (Sacks 2014). Atul Gawande's account of the death and dying of his father and the way in which it challenged his received ideas of what modern medicine can and should do is stimulating, moving and profound (Gawande 2014).

Medicine and healthcare of course lend themselves well to storytelling. Rita Charon as a physician developed a field of narrative medicine and explains what that means with numerous examples from her daily practice. She argues that doctors and other professionals 'need the expertise to listen to their patients, to understand as best they can the ordeals of illness, to honour the meanings for their patients' narratives of illness and to be moved … to act on their patients' behalf' (Charon 2008: 3). In this way, the patient-clinician consultation becomes the place where stories are forged, with patients offering up clues and fragments and professionals reading cues and subtexts to arrive at diagnoses or accounts which make sense in managing and living with their problems. She tells the moving story of a patient, Luz, who irritated the doctor with repeated demands for disability claim signatures for headaches before the uncovering of the real story of persistent family abuse.

As humans, we can relate more to the single story than the general. The skill is to select the individual example or story which illustrates and resonates with a wider message. In his book on how organisations make sense of information, Karl Weick starts himself with a powerful story (Weick 1995). He relates how long it took before the medical profession recognised harm to young children caused by deliberate parental violence. A radiologist in 1946 noted through X-rays a surprising pattern of injuries (or set of cues) which could not otherwise be explained except by intentional assault. But this hit a 'professional blind spot', with paediatricians overestimating the likelihood that they would have spotted parent-inflicted harm and radiologists not directly connected to families or doctors with direct contact with children. The original finding was published in a radiology journal not read by paediatric doctors. It was not until 1961 that there was medical recognition of 'battered child syndrome', through gathering together locally reported cases which could be seen as a pattern.

His story illustrates several themes of sense-making from professional siloes and identity to the social act of interpreting data. Weick shows how individuals and organisations use stories to illustrate and embody wider themes:

> Stories are cues within frames that are also capable of creating frames. Ideologies, paradigms, and traditions are known by their examples, not by their abstract framing principles. When people are asked to describe their ideology, they start with examples that imply patterns of belief within which these examples make sense. Stories that exemplify frames, and frames that imply stories, are two basic forms in which the substance of sensemaking becomes meaningful. (Weick 1995: 131)

There are now platforms for storytelling, like TEDx events, for researchers and scientists to reach much wider audiences. For example, check out a young Irish environmental scientist, Fergus McAuliffe, telling the story of how the wood frog freezes to life, not death. The talk itself is a masterclass in good communication.[1]

A carefully chosen story, which has wider cultural resonance, helps to connect your findings to your audience in powerful ways. In telling a story, we offer up an experience which may arouse in you interest, curiosity, pity, shame, recognition or fear. The advertising industry, using the science of persuasion and communications, understands this. In the words of Don Draper in *Mad Men*, every great ad starts with a story.

How do stories work?

In a readable account of the science of storytelling, Will Storr notes that 'story is what brain does' (Storr 2020). He identifies some essential elements of stories. One feature is change, which can cause surges of neural activity as our brains are on constant alert for potential risks or new situations where we might need to act differently. This is particularly true of unexpected change, which focuses our brain's attention on the fundamental question of story – 'what's happening?'. These dramatic turning points incite our curiosity and stimulate us to want to fill in the information gaps. This relationship between curiosity and knowledge is a critical aspect of stories and why they matter to the researcher.

To reduce it to the very basic level, stories need plot, character and setting. They also often share the element of singularity – that is 'the new, never seen'. **Plot** is not just a series of unrelated events, but the way these are ordered and linked. The engine of narrative is to find the relation and association between events. This is what Peter Brooks, in an early study of narrative fiction, described nicely as 'the organising line, the thread of design' (Brooks 1984). In a classic three-act form, this might take the shape of crisis, struggle and resolution.

There are many guides for writers analysing the structure and architecture of successful fiction. These range from the classic three-act form of crisis, struggle and resolution to Joseph

Campbell's formulation over 70 years ago of 17 archetypes or sections of plot setting out the hero's journey (Campbell 2008). But these formulae do not help the health service researcher wanting to present their findings in an engaging way. Helen Sword in her excellent primer on stylish writing for academics suggests that in telling the story of your research, you can choose how you frame it (Sword 2012). You may begin with the research question and why it matters to you (the researcher's story), a historical account of previous research (the backstory) or an example of how this research has changed lives (the impact story). At different times, you may want to use all of these lenses through which to see your research.

It helps to think of the main argument of your research. The science journalist Tim Radford has developed some guiding principles for science writers. One is that a story should only ever say one big thing. On the one hand, go big with a line of argument or organising principle. But on the other hand, stay focused on a thread. He makes a nice analogy:So if an issue is tangled like a plate of spaghetti, then regard your story as just one strand of spaghetti, carefully drawn from the whole. Ideally with the oil, garlic and tomato sauce adhering to it (Radford 2011).

In terms of stories which resonate, plot only matters when it comes into contact with **character**. As Storr notes, the job of the plot is to test the main character. This is what makes stories connect to the reader – the challenges facing characters exposes their vulnerabilities and worldviews which are flawed and individual. We are endlessly fascinated by other people and their life stories. What does this mean for the researcher? It comes down to another key principle, articulated by Jon Sutton, the editor of a psychology journal – *put the people back in*.[2] Giving human examples and personal anecdotes helps readers connect, care and be curious – enough to carry on reading to the end.

If plot and character (or human element) are essential ingredients to powerful stories, **setting** is the third factor. Good storytellers provide the reader with concrete and well-realised settings. Thomas Newman describes a campaign for infant safety seats on aeroplanes, fuelled by the first-hand account from an air steward setting the scene before an accident happened: 'It was a golden July day when disaster struck' (Newman 2003). We know from Storr that our brains are wired to evoke images and create mental models using all our senses if we are given a cue by some vivid descriptions. For researchers this might mean a personal anecdote of the environment in which data was collected or observations were taken – the beeping of machines in the intensive care ward or the hedgehog toy on the bed of a care home resident. Details matter and help to evoke a scene – the reader's imagination can do the rest. Again, in the words of Don Draper:

> The greatest thing you have working for you is not the photo you take or the picture you paint. It is the imagination of the consumer. They have no budget. They have no time limit. And if you can get into *that* space, your ad can run all day. (*Mad Men*, Season Six, Episode 4: To Have and To Hold)

Stories versus science?

There is a paradox here in the human element of stories and the power they invoke. I worked in the field of patient safety some years ago and the movement or field of knowledge was charged by a series of stories. Each one was tragic as they described individuals, often children, who had been harmed as patients in incidents which could have avoided. This included the case of Wayne Jowett, a teenager who died from a wrongful intrathecal injection while receiving chemotherapy. Martin Bromiley tells the heartbreaking story of his wife who died from a series of avoidable blunders while undergoing a minor sinus operation. The physician Thomas Newman in a powerful article (Newman 2003) describes a rare but overlooked condition of kernicterus in babies which led to the permanent and devastating disability of Susan Sheridan's son Cal. This led to an effective campaign, spearheaded by Susan Sheridan's compelling personal testimony, for screening all newborns for high bilirubin concentration.

The risks which Thomas Newman sets out are that powerful stories can overshadow the science. As he says:

> The trouble with these compelling stories is that their apparent simplicity and focus can lead to the neglect of complicated considerations of what else we might do with our resources, and how we should make these decisions. A problem for those promoting evidence based policies is that we are at a disadvantage when we cannot identify the specific people who would benefit or be harmed. (Newman 2003)

The apparent simplicity of the solution and the power of the testimony can blur the complex decisions for policy and practice. In the case of kernicterus, the context in which Cal's condition had not been identified was concern about overtreatment of neonatal jaundice in the 1990s. The corrective, prompted by stories like Cal's and medical malpractice cases, led to action which in itself bore risks of exchange transfusion and overtreatment. The answer is not to return to dry academic or technical language. Newman and others note how public health and medicine need to harness the power of stories, getting better at shaping them themselves or enlisting the help of those who do it well.

What can we learn from journalists about telling a story?

Box 8.2: Research example – air quality

Breathing better air

Some researchers build relationships with particular journalists over months or indeed years. Sir Stephen Holgate, a leading researcher and clinician on allergy and asthma, made a connection with Ben Webster, the Environment Editor for *The Times*. There were many exchanges and collaborations with a wide range of scientists and researchers. This fruitful partnership resulted in a longstanding *Times* campaign on air pollution and human health, in which the journalist scanned the national and international press to ensure a story every day on the topic. Speaking to me, Sir Stephen said, 'This campaign reached places I couldn't from my laboratory or clinic. I have worked with Ben Webster for many years and we shared a mission in improving air quality, based on the evidence. But we worked together, learning from each other.'

Journalists are skilled in setting the scene and telling a story in a way which stays with the reader. A newspaper account of the error which killed the wife of Martin Bromiley, the patient safety campaigner mentioned earlier, starts with this devastating opener:

> When Elaine Bromiley was admitted to hospital for a routine sinus operation her family kissed her goodbye and said they would see her soon. But this would be the last time they saw her conscious – Elaine, who was just 37, died 13 days after the surgery as a result of complications that could have been avoided. The mistakes by NHS staff robbed her two young children – Adam, four, and Victoria, five – of a mother and set husband Martin on a quest to change the culture of healthcare in the UK.[3]

This vividly sets the scene for the account which follows of a movement to change processes, cultures and practices in the NHS. But it starts with a human story and the everyday which turns to irreversible loss. We need to understand the pull of stories in order to be good communicators.

But researchers have responsibility to be true to the science, as well as engaging interest. The experience for a midwife of one rare but catastrophic missed diagnosis of pre-eclampsia will overshadow a hundred normal births. This is a common and well-recognised cognitive bias for us all – we remember the stories, especially those rare events with disastrous outcomes, happening to those near to us more than we do the facts on risks and probability. In my neighbourhood, the news of a woman trampled by cows while running on a route I use sticks in my mind more than the greater number of local people harmed in road traffic accidents. We need to balance the emotive appeal of stories with the wider sense of what our study means as a contribution to a body of knowledge.

Tools of persuasion

We can learn from behavioural science in understanding more about how people respond (or not) to reward, incentives and what makes them change. It is also helpful to look at evidence on persuasion and social marketing. This includes classic primers, from the 1923 handbook by top advertising man Claude C. Hopkins who invented brand images and test marketing (Hopkins 1923).[4] He also understood subliminal messaging and the power of suggestion, noting that people are best coaxed not driven. This takes a new turn in more recent work – including the new field of neuromarketing – such as *Brandwashed* by Lindstrom (Lindstrom 2012). This describes in forensic detail how companies generate and manipulate our demand for products, such as the manufactured cues of 'freshness' in Whole Foods shops. He also gives an account of the 'gamification' trend, seen in the last ten years or so, where companies adopted design principles and motivation drivers. Techniques used in games to generate incentives, rewards and competition could be used commercially to increase demand or markets. Interestingly, public health and other staff are increasingly baking in some of these approaches when designing new lifestyle change programmes (Johnson et al 2016).

Another way of framing this is captured by Larry McEnerney in an informative lecture from the University of Chicago on the craft of writing effectively.[5] He notes that writing is not to communicate your ideas, but to change your readers' ideas. Your writing only has value for (particular) readers, when they connect to the content. What does that mean as you prepare an output? Avoid putting down everything you know. Instead, focus on the reader and what matters to them. Understanding what motivates particular individuals and groups and what they want to know is a critical part of social marketing knowledge.

Using the media

We live in a digital age where the most precious commodity is attention. Indeed, there is now a growing body of thinkers and writers on the attention economy (Franck 2019). Media providers are skilled at getting our attention and keeping it. They do this by telling us stories and providing hooks which will draw us in and break up the information in a way which keeps us clicking. For some, the subject will be news, celebrities, lifestyle or politics. In other media platforms, the subject is ourselves – or carefully curated and edited versions of ourselves. In all kinds of media, the skill is in telling the stories.

Box 8.3: Interview – Clint Witchalls

Entertain and inform

I talked to Clint Witchalls, the health and medicine editor of *The Conversation*, about what makes a good story. *The Conversation* is a news service set up in the UK in 2013 (following earlier launch in Australia) with articles written by academics and researchers. Authors work with professional journalists who help to make the articles more engaging, but content comes from the people who are experts in their fields. As a news portal, content is shared with 22,000 sites worldwide giving a global reach of over 40 million readers a month.

Clint said that what makes a good story was partly the topic – the public appear to have an insatiable curiosity about neuroscience, diet, fitness and, inevitably, sex – but also the way the topic was framed. At the time of writing, top health-related stories on the website ranged from robots in care homes to whether running is bad for your knees. Plus a slew of COVID-19 related articles, from the effectiveness of corticosteroids in treating patients in hospital to the real risks to middle-aged men and likely access for different populations to effective vaccines. He suggested that researchers play to selfish interest – 'what's in it for me? How can this help me to lose weight?' without dumbing down. This might include a quirky anecdote worth passing on at dinner – 'Did you know how many words a three-year-old remembers?' – as well as headlines which describe the study and its findings – 'grammar schools do nothing for social mobility'. This is important for busy readers on mobile phones to get the gist of the story quickly. But also to optimise the chances of your study being found by people doing general searches on the internet.

Other tips from Clint include creating a line of argument, with four or five main points building up to a story – not just a string of unrelated facts. Make a compelling story with attention-grabbing statistics or quirky facts. And bring yourself in – why did you spend time on this? What findings were unexpected? What did you feel? A researcher working on calcium channels was motivated by the unexpected early death of his beloved uncle from a heart attack. In learning and understanding information, people use their senses to take in and make sense of information – so describe what the laboratory smelled like where you were working or the noise on the hospital ward when you were shadowing nursing staff in an ethnographic study.

In terms of using language, use concrete nouns rather than abstractions ('process, remuneration systems'). There is a fine balance to strike between being rightfully sensitive to concerns, for instance using phrases like 'people taking their own lives' rather than 'committing suicide' which suggests a crime. At the same time, researchers must not get too hung up on technical correctness when reaching general audiences. Clint for instance talks about tussles with academics stressing 'live virus' which may not be needed for the public at large. I remember a researcher challenging a headline we produced at our evidence centre on a non-inferiority trial where the headline suggested equivalence for two treatments. Somehow the title 'x is judged to be no worse than y under controlled circumstances' has less of a ring to it than 'x broadly the same as y'. The judgement is knowing when to let go of the last degree of accuracy in the interests of wider engagement. As Clint says, the first and last rule of journalism after all is – 'don't be boring'.

We have always known that television, newspapers and other media are very effective in amplifying and communicating research to wide audiences – and indeed, to the academic community. In an interesting analysis 30 years ago, it was found that research from a high-impact academic medical journal covered in the daily press (*The New York Times*) was twice as likely to be cited by other scholars (Phillips et al 1991). This effect was not apparent during the period of a strike by the newspaper, providing a natural experiment to study the effect of newspaper coverage on citation rates. The power of the media to enhance the impact of research has been given extra charge in recent years with the growth of social media platforms and activities.

Using social media

Researchers who want to reach wider audiences need to develop skills and competence in using social media. There is good science to indicate the effect that social media can have. For instance, a trial on the use of Twitter relating to Cochrane schizophrenia reviews showed more visits to review pages (Adams et al 2016). Importantly, readers also stayed longer reading the research when directed by accurate Twitter messages rather than stumbling across the research online. If you want to communicate your findings well, social media is an important set of tools at your disposal.

There are useful guides on making the most of new media channels, from Facebook to LinkedIn to Twitter. For social science and health researchers, helpful resources include the toolkit for communicating research produced in 2017 by the Health Foundation www.health.org.uk/publications/communicating-your-research-a-toolkit and the Economic and Social Research Council (ESRC) guide to social media for researchers https://esrc.ukri.org/research/impact-toolkit/social-media/using-social-media/.

Twitter is one of the most useful platforms for academics to engage more widely. Many people start by following a number of influencers and 'lurking' before they send posts themselves. You need to find the influencers and people whose threads you find interesting, trying to broaden your range to include diverse opinions and those outside your professional tribe. It is useful to forward and comment on other tweets and content, as well as generating your own content. Those who only 'broadcast' their own output, or promote their own organisation, are not making the most of Twitter or being a generous member of the online community. A good rule is to only post one tweet about your own work to every four or five where you are liking, responding to and sharing content of others. It can also be a valuable resource to ask questions and crowdsource information or identify new experts. The best opinion leaders on Twitter signpost material from a wide range of sources, offer opinion and connect people from different spheres.

Twitter can also be a source of 'play' and creativity. I saw a thread started by Emma Nuding, a medieval scholar at York University in June 2020 where people were asked to summarise their PhD theses in four words (see Figure 8.1). Different responses caught my eye and left me wanting to read more.

Using humour, surprise and curiosity is a feature of good communication. In April 2020 during the first stage of the pandemic, Doncaster Council had a Twitter campaign reinforcing the need to follow government advice to stay at home during lockdown. The tweets told a seemingly unrelated history lesson of how 50 years earlier Oregon officials had struggled to remove a rotting whale carcass from a public beach. In a thread of 11 tweets, with humorous video and images, it told the story with a message which hit home – 'don't ignore expert advice'. It achieved more than 130,000 impressions (likes, retweets and comments) with a total engagement over April above 4 million and over 13,000 new followers to @ MyDoncaster. Not bad for a corporate account selling a public health message.

As the term suggests, the essence of social media is that it is social. Rather than just seeing Twitter or other platforms as a way of sharing or broadcasting your work, you need to engage and make connections with people. It is a social process. In Chapter 4, I mentioned the work of Teresa Chinn (Box 4.7) who set up the @WeNurses Twitter account, which now attracts nearly 100,000 followers who are mainly nurses. The platform is a lively mix of links to useful resources, information and facilitated Tweetchats on big issues of the day, from burnout to breaking bad news. It also drives social media campaigns, such as an initiative to support nurses getting more active and looking after themselves. Teresa, who is herself a great communicator, talks about the 'reciprocal acts' of engaging on Twitter and

Figure 8.1: Twitter as a source of creativity

Source: Permission given by each of above via Twitter – 24 October 2020.

makes a point of replying personally to each tweet and keeping the conversation going. For her, one of the ways in which she connects with nurses on Twitter is by celebrating people and activities as well as informing, sharing and learning. This might mean telling stories about a difficult day working in a care home or completing a master's while looking after small children.

Authentic connection – bringing your whole self in (or at least a good part of it) – is key to keeping people engaged.

A useful resource is the kudos platform (www.growkudos.com), launched in 2013 as a free service for researchers. It works by creating 'profiles' for your published articles and makes it easier to share your findings and track impact on social media. The activities of this platform are three-fold:

- Explain: researchers are asked to write two simple paragraphs about their study: 'What is it about?' and 'Why is it important?'
- Share: for each study profiled, the platform helps researcher to share content across social media and links across discovery channels (like search engines and subject indexes) so it can be found more easily.
- Measure: article-level metrics from number of people downloading the paper, citations, tweets and interaction on social media plus other measures of impact.

Your university and organisation communication departments will provide other valuable advice on promoting and targeting your work. In our evidence centre, our communications team taught me a lot about audience segmentation, marketing and digital communications. In particular, they changed how we framed our evidence summaries, looking for ways of making them more likely to be found in online searches. This is known as Search Engine Optimisation or SEO and by using tagging and keywords, you can increase what is called the 'organic search traffic', that is, people finding your paper by putting in a general query on Google or similar. Academics like Bev Holmes have noted the overlooked importance of strategic communications in disseminating and promoting research (Holmes et al 2017). In a rapidly changing world, communication teams are likely to have more up-to-date knowledge on social media behaviours for particular target audiences. Is Facebook, LinkedIn, Instagram or Twitter most popular for who you want to reach? Ask your communications colleagues for help in framing and tagging your research to broaden – or indeed, target more narrowly – your digital audience.

It is also important to keep visible and maintain your personal profile as a researcher. You can use research identifiers like ORCID to link you and your outputs to any related discussion or online activity. You may also want to think about creating a visual identity for your project and an attractive project website. This could include important research outputs, including summaries, but may include other material such as a recorded webinar on YouTube. You can share conference presentations or posters using repositories like SlideShare, Figshare or Zenodo. While these will probably be used mainly by other researchers, you can think about wider engagement at science festivals, TEDx talks, roadshows, science slams or science cafes.

You can evaluate any new approach you try by using analytics, easily available for any platform. This will give you a sense of who you are reaching (number of downloads or post/link clicks); their response (number of likes, comments, replies or retweets); and rates of engagement (the proportion of likes/comments to the total number of times a tweet or post is seen). In social media marketing terms, a rate of 1 per cent is seen as good in terms of engagement. Get used to trying new formats, using photographs or data visualisation tools, and monitoring and evaluating what difference this makes to your digital footprint. Mastering the basic tools of social media is important for an engaged scholar in the 21st century. But you can start by small steps. On a platform like Twitter, follow other people who have something interesting to say and notice what works well. You can try out a few tweets using different formats and content to see which stimulate interest and debate.

Using a range of media

Different kinds of media channels and formats can be used to get across the main findings of your study to different audiences in different ways. One health services research project (Box 8.4) made use of a range of media to share findings about the experience of hospital patients with dementia.

Box 8.4: Research example – understanding inpatients with dementia

Refusing care and how it happens

One health services research project used a range of media channels and formats to tell the story of their research. This was a three-year observational study led by Katie Featherstone at Cardiff University in which researchers shadowed staff and patients in hospital wards (Featherstone et al 2019). The aim was to find out more about the ways in which patients living with dementia 'resisted' everyday care, from food to medicines, and included staff perspectives to identify what ward staff might be able to do differently. The study found that patients living with dementia frequently refused essential drugs or fluids. Sometimes they actively resisted, for instance pulling out intravenous lines or catheters. But researchers noted that standard ward routines and the containment practices by staff – whether repeating instructions in loud voices or raising side rails to confine patients to beds – often triggered greater resistance and anxiety in patients living with dementia. Researchers observed these damaging cycles of stress and their impacts on patients and families and ward staff. They also noted that ward staff often attributed resistance to the condition of dementia itself, rather than the responses of individuals to the organisation and delivery of their care.

This research was shared in a number of ways. A prime target audience were busy ward staff themselves, with practical take-home messages to improve care. The researchers worked with dementia specialist nurses and general ward staff to develop and implement some simple interventions at ward level, for calming and responding to individual needs of patients living with dementia. But the researchers also wanted to reach people with dementia, families and carers, and the general public. Given that over a quarter of hospital patients also have dementia, most of us will have relatives or friends living with dementia who need hospital care. Katie Featherstone, the lead investigator, worked with contacts in film and media to produce short films of people living with dementia and carers talking about their experiences of a hospital admission, and vignettes of patient and staff interaction on wards as training resources. Content was also produced in films of under a minute for use on Facebook,

Instagram, and Twitter and shared at annual festivals during dementia awareness week. These short films were also used to bring alive the research findings, which led to the final report being featured on the BBC and other national and regional television and radio, as well as a range of print broadsheet feature articles and coverage in professional press. In turn, this led to the Department of Health and Welsh Government providing written statements in response to the research. This whole ambitious programme of communication and engagement was overseen by a network of around 50 patients, carers and ward staff, who supported the research programme.

The art of blogging

The blog or blog post is an informal article which is a great way to tell the story of your research. Blogs are informal, conversational, entertaining. Academic blogging platforms, like *The Conversation* https://theconversation.com/uk (Box 8.3) for all kinds of research or Mental Elf (www.nationalelfservice.net/mental-health/) for more targeted interest, provide curated sites for researchers to post interesting content on their research. Individuals can also set up their own blogging sites using software like Blogger (http://blogger.com/) or WordPress (http://wordpress.com/), but will have to take active steps to create and sustain audiences. You can also post guest blogs through your university or with partner service organisations and networks in your field. Multi-author and group blogs are a good way of reaching across disciplines and breaking down siloes of knowledge (Dunleavy and Tinkler 2020) although there are trade-offs between strengths of collaboration and dilution of personal voice.

There are no set rules for blogs, which range from unstructured opinion pieces to forms like 'listicles'. This has become rather hackneyed, but often does the job in attracting reader attention, by organising your findings in list form such as 'Ten things you didn't know about what works in improving life chances for care leavers'. Although there is no absolute wordcount limit, blogs are best when relatively short, at around 600–800 words. They are often framed around personal accounts or anecdotes, single threads of interest and connections across subjects. The form is aimed at general debate and readers, so most avoid references or add embedded links to source material. But good blogs rest on the authority and voice of the writer, so over-generalised statements without foundation should be avoided.

As Clint Witchalls noted (Box 8.3), unexpected facts or nuggets of information can be useful to draw the reader in and start the story. Blogs also often use paradox and reversal. This for instance is a post I wrote on the importance of social science research at a time of pandemic – but opens with a (real) story undermining its importance:

> I remember being at an academic gathering of healthcare social scientists a few years back. A lot of withering talk of the dominant paradigm of biomedical research and the limitations of positivist thinking. Then one of the delegates had a heart attack. Complete panic until someone said, 'I'm a doctor, a real doctor', and not one of those proud sociologists demurred. I'm glad to say, the person recovered, in no small part due to the quick attention of the physician. But we all felt a bit humbled. It was hard to see how an epistemic framework could have saved a person's life.[6]

The great advantage of the blog is that the researcher can control the content. This minimises risk of distortion or spin. But there is an art to good blogging, and those starting out can work with journalists and others to get feedback and learn how to both entertain and inform.

Picture worth a thousand words

It is increasingly important to think **visuals** when telling the story of your research. A recent book (Engebretsen and Kennedy 2020) looks at the way in which pictures, maps and innovative graphic forms can bring to life complex data. This can help in conveying multiple relations of data on space, population, health and behaviours in an efficient way. It is also a way 'to produce meanings, feelings and engagement' (Engebretsen and Kennedy 2020: 22). People tend to think of graphs and computer-generated images based on big data of different forms. But some of the most powerful use of data visualisation is hand-drawn, such as that used by the data journalist Mona Chalabi (www.monachalabi.com). Her detailed and beautiful drawing of a hundred New York residents, true to the demographic data, their risk of COVID-19 infection and the interplay between race, poverty, overcrowding and other factors conveys much complex information in an elegant and engaging way. This may be beyond most of us, but researchers can check out free resources such as DataHero, Canva or Plotly and play around with different ways of presenting results which are accurate and arresting.

Infographics are a way of summarising headline findings and graphics in a single chart. These can present complex data in a visual way and can be shared easily on social media. As with text, economy is all – identifying one or two 'killer facts' which illustrate the central argument is as important as the artistry. There are some nice examples by thinktanks and government departments, including the bold and arresting graphics from Public Health England illustrating the cost to the economy of lower back pain (Figure 8.2).

Imaginative ways of telling stories are not just about slick packaging and use of arresting infographics, animations or memes. The medium needs to be appropriate for the message and the audience. In earlier chapters, I looked at particular channels and platforms for reaching particular target audiences, including partnership with professional bodies to get research to practitioners. Identifying and tagging important online communities of advocacy groups, patients, professionals or policy analysts is essential for targeted and effective communication strategies. But as well as this targeted activity, social media is also a great way of reaching a range of people who might not otherwise come across your research. To do this, you need to distil your findings into a compelling message. And find the story which will make them want to read more.

Figure 8.2: Use of infographics

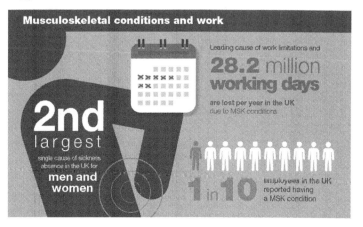

Source: Public Health England (2019) Health matters: health and work – GOV.UK (www.gov. uk). Reproduced with permission.

PRACTICAL POINTERS FOR USING MEDIA AND STORIES

Write a blog

Write a blog on your research in an anecdotal or conversational style. You might want to tell a personal story explaining your original motivation to do the research or recall an encounter or visit during your fieldwork which struck you or some struggle in the course of the project which stimulated new thinking. Bring in the sounds and sights and smells where you can. Make it all about the people. Add some compelling facts or data – anything unusual or unexpected? Start with the main point of interest and then expand. Keep sentences and paragraphs short and make the piece easy to scan. Link to relevant images, videos and other multimedia content, as well as source references but keep the text clean and simple. You want to start a conversation, so ask readers questions and respond to comments. Before you post a blog, share it with a friend or colleague – or better still, an editor or journalist or communications officer – and revise.

Tweet all about it

Make a headline of your main findings – or a short tweet of no more than 140 characters. Then go one step further and summarise your study in a tweet of just four words, making it as playful as possible. Construct the story of your research as a tweet thread, with 6–10 individual tweets ordered to follow a line of argument. Tag people who may be interested and use hashtags to relate content to relevant online discussion and events. Monitor the effect of this, using analytics to see if people retweeted, commented or visited your source research paper or project website.

Stand up and talk

Create a TED talk of 18 minutes or less (preferably less) about your research. Try one version without any slides or visuals. Open with an anecdote or personal story. Start big or start small. Watch other talks to see how effective presentations are structured (even if they appear not to be). There is no single style, but it is striking how some of the most viewed talks appear to go against the grain of what we think of as effective public speaking. What the speakers have in common is they are authentic and true to themselves and are enthusiastic about their subject. People often use humour and connect to the audience with common experience, but also insert surprising and unexpected information. Think about starting with a paradoxical image or fact. Keep in mind three top line findings from your research which you want the audience to remember. Don't overload the audience with detail and data. Structure the talk, perhaps ending with a return to the opening premise now seen in a different light.

9

HOW to reach people – finding the right language and style

Summary

This chapter looks at questions of style in reaching wider audiences. It starts with one of the most important aspects of communicating your research, using accessible language and writing effective plain language summaries. I consider some of the commonly agreed precepts of good writing style, drawing on work by recent academics to push the boundaries of what it means to write well as a researcher. I set out eight important features in good writing which go beyond grammar and basic style rules. This includes thinking about the title of your work; writing as you speak, avoiding the convolutions of academic thought; identifying main messages and expressing them clearly; being as true as you can to the science and avoiding over-claiming and spin; being playful; using tricks of persuasion; choosing words carefully; and finally, perhaps most importantly, finding your voice. More guidance and books on style are given in the Further reading section, and the chapter ends with three practical pointers to writing for impact. Finding the appropriate tone, language and idiom for different audiences and outputs is difficult and needs effort. The best way to learn is to take note of people and places which do this well and practise yourself.

Writing plain language summaries

This book is about how to communicate research findings to audiences who are not researchers. Perhaps the most important tool to do this is the plain language summary. This is likely to be the most read output and yet is often done as an afterthought. More time is needed to get this right, working with others – particularly people who know nothing about your research. This chapter looks at the language and format to reach wide audiences, starting with the plain language summary as a critical part of your pathway to impact.

We all know it is important to avoid jargon and technical words. This means replacing peripheral oedema with ankle swelling and avoiding terms like *in vitro* which are not in everyday use. The aim is to use simple, clear language. But it is very difficult to do, especially if your research is complex and nuanced. As Einstein may have said[1] – 'keep it as simple as possible, but no simpler'.

There is a useful paper by Rob Waller, who set up a charity – The Simplification Centre – from Reading University on making information more accessible (Waller 2011). He emphasises that writing simply is not dumbing down and provides some useful strategies for making work clearer. He busts some myths – for instance, to put text into plain language may make some reports longer, not shorter. Jargon works because it is a shorthand between professionals, but it is not understood by all. Opening up text for wider understanding is a political point. The Simplification Centre, like the pioneering work of Chrissie Maher and the Plain English Campaign, was started with a mission to open up the worlds of law, consumer rights, benefits and health information to more people.

In health-related research, good work has been done by the Cochrane collaboration in developing plain language summaries. It is difficult to make complex findings accessible, without distorting the science. An audit some time ago of plain language summaries by the Cochrane team found that almost a third were inaccurate in relation to the main findings in the full review or abstract and could be misleading (Soares-Weiser 2011). This included elements like presenting treatment effects in relative terms ('the risks were doubled') without giving a sense of the absolute numbers ('from one in a hundred thousand to two in a hundred thousand'). Much work is being done on how to present information in a responsible and accurate way. This includes iterative work with consumers to test and refine Cochrane public summaries in a rigorous way (Synnot et al 2018).

Earlier studies showed that readers often did not understand summaries of research developed for public use by Cochrane review groups. For instance, a randomised trial of 143 members of the public from different countries compared different formats of plain language summaries, measuring reader understanding of benefits and harms of the intervention and research quality (Santesso et al 2015). Only one in five (18 per cent) readers understood the traditional format, increasing to 53 per cent for a newer version. While an improvement, it is not a great endorsement of a public-facing summary that only just over half of people reading it understood the main points. A similar proportion of the public understood findings in a smaller study, with just over half understanding the findings in a plain language summary, which was an improvement on the scientific abstract alone which only a third understood (Maguire and Clarke 2014). Cochrane review groups and staff have spent much time on this, with useful how-to guides on writing plain language summaries (Glenton 2017) and a recent consensus checklist on how to report clearly and accurately the effects of interventions (Oxman et al 2020). These present helpful advice, although geared more to clinical effectiveness studies and systematic reviews than the full range of study designs in health and social care research.

In short, even with much effort, it is still very difficult to write summaries which are accurate and accessible. But however imperfect, they tend to be much easier to understand than scientific abstracts and other research outputs. At their best, public-facing summaries can distil the key messages of your research in an economical way. But this takes time and multiple iterations to get right. You need to think about the plain language summary as an important output in its own right, not just remove a few hard words. Rob Waller points helpfully to the work of Widdowson (1979) who distinguishes between 'simplified versions' and 'simple accounts'. Waller notes the importance of this distinction:

> The former are translations of existing documents, while the latter are documents that are originally planned, written and designed to be easy to understand. Most documents intended for children are simple accounts: both content and form are created from the outset with that audience in mind. It is an important distinction, because it reflects a different dynamic of production. (Waller 2011)

That is, you need to start with a blank sheet of paper to construct a public-facing simple summary, rather than water down an abstract for a scientific journal changing a few words here and there. It is the difference between word for word translations or Google Translate and the work of a skilled interpreter, fluent in both languages.

There are no easy rules or prescription for writing summaries which are accessible and accurate. It is a craft and needs a combination of skills. What we found at our evidence centre was that it was best thought of as a process where many could contribute. That included science writers and journalists, those with critical appraisal skills (understanding the findings and strength of evidence, including possible risk of bias) and people with lived experience as staff or patients. This is an iterative process. The earlier chapter on patients and the public gave an example from our work with an advocacy group to co-produce an easy-read version of a research report with people with learning disabilities (Figure 5.5).

Tools are available to test how easy it is to read your text. Two common tools, measuring length of sentences and words, are the Gunning Fog index developed in the 1940s and the Flesch-Kincaid levels in the 1970s. There are free online services to calculate the readability of your text against these specified levels measured by educational level (in the US). The general aim would be to make papers accessible for students aged 13 to 15 years. These automated tools are helpful, but cannot give you all the answers. Some long words with many syllables are commonly used and understood. Some short words are obscure or formal. There also may be particular audiences you want to reach, like clinical staff or managers. For target readers, some jargon or technical terms can provide context and clarity. Using readability tools can be mechanistic and will not tell you if a summary is clear about why a study is important and what it found. Rules used by algorithms, such as use of adverbs or intensifiers being a marker of poor style, do not always hold good.

Skimming through the NIHR research portfolio, I selected two examples which I think are good plain language summaries, although their reading score age profiles are in the mid to high teens (Box 9.1). But they do the job for me in conveying complex research findings as simply as they can and explaining why the research is important. They also don't go further than the study design allows – for instance, the second example in Box 9.1 is a feasibility study and so findings are suitably cautious. The best rule when you write a simple summary is whether a friend or neighbour can easily understand the research and relay back to you what it is all about and why it matters. Tools can't do this for you.

Box 9.1: Plain language summaries – two examples

'Telephone first' general practices (Newbould et al 2019)

Every one of us wants to be able to visit our family doctor when needed. With so many more patients, this is becoming increasingly difficult. The study looked at a new way to ask for help from one's doctor to see if this would save overall time and NHS money. Patients were asked to speak first to a GP or doctor by telephone to see if their problem could be dealt with over the telephone or if they needed to see the doctor in person. Practices using the 'telephone first' approach were compared with other practices that were not using it.

In a patient survey, it was shown that just over half of patients found it easier to make appointments with the 'telephone first' approach than with the previous system, with nearly one quarter finding it less easy or the same. It was quicker to make an appointment in those practices using this new way, but, when asked, patients and practice staff had strong views both for and against the new system. Factors affecting patient satisfaction included the ease of getting through to the general practice on the telephone and how easy it was to wait for the callback from the GP (for example if the patient was at work).

'Telephone first' greatly increased the number of doctor consultations by telephone, with around half of problems managed in this way. This led to more work for practice staff, although there were big differences between practices, with some having much more work and others having much less. There was not much difference in the use of hospital services or in the costs of hospital care.

Although the study showed that, by using the 'telephone first' approach, many health problems can be dealt with over the telephone, this will not solve the increasing need for care by our family doctors.

Trying new approaches to sex education in schools (Mitchell et al 2020)

Young people report higher levels of unsafe sex and have higher rates of sexually transmitted infections than any other age group. Good sex education is important for later sexual health, but it needs to be done well. We tested an approach to sex education (called the Sexually Transmitted infections And Sexual Health (STASH) intervention) in which influential students – chosen by their year group – were trained to start conversations with other students about sexual health on social media and face to face. This approach has previously worked well to prevent young people taking up smoking. Working with students, teachers, health professionals and youth workers, we adapted the approach for sexual health and older students (aged 14–16 years).

We also developed a website of digital resources (memes, infographics, web links, and so on) that could be shared via social media. We tested the approach in one school, made adjustments and then delivered it in six schools in Scotland. We wanted to find out if it was practical to deliver and whether or not those taking part would like it. We observed some of the project activities, kept careful track of participation, interviewed students and teachers, and asked peer supporters to complete a brief web survey. We also asked the whole year group to fill in a questionnaire about their sexual attitudes and behaviour, and about taking part in the STASH study. We compared their answers with those of students in the year above who had completed the questionnaire the previous year.

About half of the students who were chosen as 'most influential' by their friends decided to become peer supporters. Once trained, nearly all of those chosen completed the role and many of them were active on social media and in conversations. Students and teachers generally liked the project. Using social media (closely monitored by adult trainers) was helpful and did not cause problems. Our findings suggest that it would be worth doing a larger study to find out if the STASH intervention can increase the number of young people staying safe from sexually transmitted infections (either by always using condoms or by not having sex).

What do we mean by writing well?

There is reasonable consensus on what we mean by good writing. Numerous style guides (see Further reading for some key texts) point to the importance of the following features:

- keep it clear and simple – avoid technical jargon and keep writing as concise as possible, using plain English terms;
- use active verbs – avoid passive forms ('it has been demonstrated that') and nominalisation, where verbs are turned into nouns in a formal style ('articulation', 'marginalisation');
- shorten sentences – keep sentences short or mix longer with shorter sentences;
- be precise – use examples and avoid generalities.

But in an arresting book by the academic Helen Sword, she notes how rarely this advice is followed in scholarly outputs (Sword 2012). Taking a thousand academic articles from different disciplines, she audited them against the checklist of good writing. Few of them satisfied these base requirements. She found that many were written in a convoluted, indirect, formal style with long sentences and abstractions. Results from this small sample confounded some preconceptions about different fields of study. Some of the humanities performed less well than fields like computer science in terms of their use of active verbs or personal pronouns.

To the general advice on good use of language, Helen Sword added other features from her scan of a hundred authors nominated by 70 colleagues as good and stylish academic writers. These additional elements included:

- eye-catching titles;
- arresting opening, with an engaging story or challenging question;
- first-person anecdotes or asides that give a sense of the author;
- numerous examples to explain abstract terms or theory;
- visual illustrations beyond standard graphs;
- references to broad and wide-ranging sources beyond the narrow field of enquiry;
- humour, whether overt or implicit.

She found evidence of these traits in academic articles, as well as more public-facing books by scholars. One of her conclusions is that academics constrain themselves into a formal style at odds with the precepts of good writing. They internalise 'rules' which they think are required in order to get published. Helen Sword's work shows that there is space for invention and creativity even within the constraints of academic publishing. But increasingly, researchers are looking to publish not only in academic journals. They also want to reach wider audiences beyond the library and common room. For these audiences, used to engaging and sophisticated offerings for entertainment and information, it is important that you tell your story well.

Some pointers are given in this chapter to improve the way you present your research, with some summary tips at the end. It is also important to tailor outputs to particular audiences. Issues of format and language appropriate to frontline clinical staff or community groups or government advisers were covered in earlier chapters (Chapters 4–6).

Writing for impact

Box 9.2: Writing for impact – key features

- start well
- be natural – or write as you speak
- get to the point
- stay true to the science
- be playful
- be persuasive
- choose words carefully
- be yourself – the importance of voice

In what follows I identify eight important features when writing for impact, with some background, examples and a few practical pointers at the end so that you can develop a style which works for you.

Start well

A good title can both inform and engage the reader. While some scientific journals have minimum requirements – information about study design for indexing and transparency, there is still freedom to inject a bit of humour, surprise or liveliness. I mentioned my search for good titles on Twitter, and a number of researchers said they had had their suggestions for more playful titles rejected by journal editors, who amended them to more factual titles. This is not always true of publishers and editors (as Box 9.3 shows), so it is worth persisting in the hope of greater audience interest and reach.

I carried out my own exercise, scanning one year of six health services research journals to identify the titles which appealed to me – a subjective exercise – plus a few additional ones suggested by friends and contacts on Twitter (Box 9.3). It strikes me that qualitative research has an advantage, with many using well-selected informant quotes and data extracts to add colour to the header. There is of course a fine line between the eye-catching and the irritating, particularly when certain tropes get over-used (for instance, 'if X is the answer, what is the question?') A few puns can go a long way. Helen Sword (2012) has some good tips for researchers in her chapter on titles, including avoiding over-use of the colon in lengthy titles. This is particularly true when both parts of the title, separated by a colon, are purely descriptive, rather than an engaging: informative structure.

Box 9.3: Titles which pull readers in

These were recent titles from health services research journals which made me curious and want to read more.

'Partnership or insanity: why do health partnerships do the same thing over and over again and expect a different result?'

'How wide is the Goldilocks Zone in your health system?'

'"This is our liver patient …": use of narratives during resident and nurse handoff conversations'

'The view from nowhere? How thinktanks work to shape health policy'

'Systematic reviews of economic evaluations: utility or futility?'

'Health system goals: life, death … and football'

'Variations in healthcare: the good, the bad and the inexplicable'

'Psychotherapy Research Evidence and Reimbursement Decisions: Bambi Meets Godzilla'

Be natural – or write as you speak

Peter Elbow, a professor of English at the University of Massachusetts Amherst, wrote a powerful piece on what he calls 'academic disability' (Elbow 2013). It is worth quoting a passage in full, as he describes so well the way in which academic writing becomes convoluted and dense. He states:

> When we academics were in graduate school, we were trained to write badly (no one put it this way of course) because every time we wrote X, our teacher always commented, 'But have you considered Y? Don't you see that Y completely contradicts what you write here.' 'Have you considered' is the favourite knee-jerk response of academics to any idea. As a result, we learn as students to clog up our writing with added clauses and phrases to keep them from being attacked … As a result of all this training we come to internalize these written voices so that they speak to us continually from inside our own heads. So even when we talk and start to say 'X,' we interrupt ourselves to say 'Y,' but then turn around and say 'Nevertheless X in certain respects, yet nevertheless Y in other respects.' We end up with our minds tied in knots.

He goes on to defend this as a marker of what he calls:

> a valuable habit of mind. It's the habit of always hearing and considering a different idea or conflicting view while engaged in saying anything. Too many things seem to go on at once in our minds; we live with constant interruptions and mental invasions as we speak. We are trained as academics to look for exceptions, never to accept one idea or point of view or formulation without looking for contradictions or counter examples or opposing ideas. Yet this habit gets so internalized that we often don't quite realize we are doing it; we just 'talk normally' – but this normal is fractured discourse to listeners.

What he argues is that we need to *un-learn* some of these good habits in order to communicate clearly and well to non-academic audiences. It is not that academics can't write and think clearly and effectively. It is that scholars are hard-wired to qualify, justify and pose counter-arguments which leads to convoluted and stodgy prose.

His prescription is simple and effective. Read your work out loud. It forces shorter, clearer sentences and natural rhythms of speech. If it is difficult to say, chances are the sentences are too long or the syntax is too complex. Often long sentences, which become paragraphs, have a lot of words between the subject and verb. A good rule of thumb, which happens naturally when you speak, is to keep the main verb close to the object near the start of a sentence. When you don't, it becomes difficult to say or understand. '*Clinical staff*, already enacting many of these paradoxes in their workarounds without knowingly breaching the normative rules of engagement, or at least without articulation of these transgressions in habituated practice, *do not* always conform to expected patterns of behaviour.' Reading this clumsy sentence (which I made up) out loud would make you stop to take breath and try to make sense of the meaning by clearer, shorter statements. Reading out loud is a great rule for all kinds of writing, but particularly when you are trying to reach general or wider audiences.

Get to the point

Tim Radford, a former science editor for *The Guardian*, had useful advice for journalists writing feature articles. 'A story will only ever say one big thing. Summarise it in one sentence' (Radford 2011). That is a good precept for researchers preparing a version of their findings. More attention should be spent on headline findings than on anything else. Crafting a single sentence which gives the main findings while staying true to the science is difficult. But that is what the reader will take away.

In our evidence centre, we spent a lot of time drafting and redrafting the titles of our research summaries (Box 9.3). We wanted them to be bold and declarative, without over-simplifying. We were particularly aware of the risks of over-claiming for single studies and giving weight to the quality of evidence, risk of bias and level of certainty. But we wanted clear headline findings. Note in the examples in Box 9.4, the conclusions in scientific papers quite rightly need to provide accurate and detailed findings and explain the 'workings' to support conclusions. Nevertheless, it is sometimes difficult for readers to understand at a glance the findings of a study.

Box 9.4: Summary headlines – from academic to journalistic

Headline: 'Adding a third antiplatelet drug after a stroke doesn't reduce the risk of another stroke' (NIHR 2018)[2]

Original conclusions: We aimed to compare the safety and efficacy of intensive antiplatelet therapy (combined aspirin, clopidogrel and dipyridamole) with that of guideline-based antiplatelet therapy ... In this cohort of patients with acute, non-cardioembolic ischaemic stroke or TIA, a regimen of intensive antiplatelet therapy did not reduce stroke recurrence or its severity when compared with guideline antiplatelet therapy with either clopidogrel alone or combined aspirin and dipyridamole. (Bath et al 2017)

Headline: 'Group-based interventions may help teenagers stop smoking' (NIHR 2018)[3]

Original conclusions: Forty-one trials involving more than 13,000 young people met our inclusion criteria (26 individually randomised controlled trials and 15 cluster-randomised trials). Interventions were varied, with the majority adopting forms of individual or group counselling, with or without additional self-help materials to form complex interventions. Eight studies used primarily computer or messaging interventions, and four small studies used pharmacological interventions (nicotine patch or gum, or bupropion). There was evidence of an intervention effect for group counselling (nine studies, risk ratio (RR) 1.35, 95 per cent confidence interval (CI) 1.03 to 1.77), but not for individual counselling (seven studies, RR 1.07, 95 per cent CI 0.83 to 1.39), mixed delivery methods (eight studies, RR 1.26, 95 per cent CI 0.95 to 1.66) or the computer or messaging interventions (pooled RRs between 0.79 and 1.18, nine studies in total). (Fanshawe et al 2017)

Up until the end of 2017, the limit for a tweet was 140 characters. It was then doubled, but when we were creating headlines for our evidence summaries, we kept to the original limit as shorter is (almost always) better. Having a title or headline finding which can easily be tweeted is useful in promoting through social media channels. Limiting the number of words is a good discipline, which is worth adopting.

Stay true to the science

There is a fine line between simple, compelling accounts of your work and exaggerating the impact of a single study. Paying attention to language, means avoiding spin. Good work has been done by Petroc Sumner and colleagues at Cardiff University in exposing and understanding the nature of spin in science. Their work at InSciOut (sites.cardiff.ac.uk/insciout/) has shown how university press releases and press coverage can misrepresent findings. This does not always come from sloppy reporting by journalists – their study in 2016 showed that much of the exaggeration found in health and science stories came from university press releases themselves, perhaps reflecting recent drive to maximise impact in a competitive world (Sumner et al 2016).

Another study looked at how findings can be misrepresented. Analysis showed how a third of press releases and four out of five news stories contained causal claims when the research papers described correlation (Sumner et al 2014). This kind of distortion can be seen in just one recent example (Box 9.4).[4]

Box 9.5: Research example – green spaces

One thing leads to another

Let's just take one recent example of distorted accounts of research findings in the general media. An observational study published in *Nature* in 2019 used self-reported data from over 20,000 adults surveyed in the UK. This showed a relationship between exposure to green spaces and wellbeing. The authors were interested in looking at the 'dose-response' and made cautious assertions that there appeared to be a threshold of benefits at 120 minutes' exposure a week, peaking at about 200–300 minutes after which little additional benefit was seen. They emphasised that 'the tentative "threshold" and peak [are] discussed here more as a starting point for discussion and further investigation, than clearly established findings' (White et al 2019).

Perhaps predictably, this was widely covered in popular and general media as well as the scientific press. In a sea of doom, the good news that spending just a couple of hours outdoors in nature could be good for you was compelling. Two errors appeared in much of the coverage. The first was the confusion of causality and association – this study was only looking at the relationship between various factors and wellbeing. For instance, one online news headline stated confidently: 'Spending 2 hours in nature each week can make you happier and health, study says' (Gravier 2019).

The second problem was the categorical nature of the two-hour threshold and how this was reported in some parts of the media. *The New York Times* for instance had a bold header, 'How Much Nature Is Enough? 120 Minutes a Week, Doctors Say' (Sheikh 2019). The article talked of an ideal amount of time, suggesting even that two hours might be a ceiling ('enough') rather than a tentative threshold level, as the authors stated.

But it is not all bad news. Researchers from InSciOut used their rigorous methods to show, encouragingly, that science reported responsibly and well can still garner headlines and column inches (or the equivalent in social media terms). Rachel Adams and colleagues carried out a trial in which they compared regular press outputs with 'evidence-based' press releases where headlines were aligned with supporting evidence and conclusions were caveated, particularly being more cautious if findings were around associations not causal links. They found that the press releases which were true to the science had just as much press coverage as those which were less accurate (Adams et al 2019).

Be playful

A book came out ten years ago which was – sort of – a novel, but formed only of questions. There were no characters, no plot, just a series of questions. 'Are you a circusgoer? Do you like to lick stamps? … Do children smell good? … Between an automobile mechanic and a psychologist, which is worth more to you per hour? … If it might be fairly said that you have hopes and fears, would you say you had more hopes than fears or more fears than hopes?' The effect was mesmerising, juxtaposing the banal with the profound in strange and often moving ways. It was startlingly original and made me think again about what makes for a connection between writer and reader. It is worth checking out in full – *The Interrogative Mood* by Padgett Powell (2010).

A good test of the ideas and findings and argument running through your research is to try out different ways of presenting them. Not perhaps through creative dance or shadowplay. But it may be that you can unlock some of the threads of your research through a series of pen-portraits, vignettes, images or questions.

Be persuasive

There is still a lot to learn from the ancient masters. A recent study of rhetoric (Leith 2012) uncovered how politicians and great speechmakers use – consciously or unconsciously – the lessons of persuasion identified from Aristotle onwards. That includes combining the three branches of oratory: ethos (establishing the credibility of the speaker); logos (setting out a powerful line of argument, with reason and logic); and pathos (appealing to the emotions). A researcher telling the story of their study will need at different times to invoke all three, although on the surface perhaps only addressing the logos or main findings. To connect with the audience or reader, it helps to remind them of who you are and why you have authority to speak – as one of them or as someone with experience and expertise to share. A clinical researcher addressing healthcare audiences may start with an anecdote from their own practice or talk about the hours spent shadowing staff on the wards on this study. Injecting some emotion may mean invoking the particular – the sights, smells, sounds of those wards for you as a researcher or that of an inpatient with dementia 'resisting' active medical care.

For researchers, the art of persuasion is not just understanding what drives people or asserting an argument. It is also placing your work in the wider evidence base. A useful book by Graff and Birkenstein states that 'writing well means entering a conversation summarising others ("they say") to set up one's own argument ("I say")'. The authors use templates or hooks to help researchers to structure their line of debate – 'while some argue that, I think this …'. This is a useful structuring device to make your case persuasively while recognising the wider tradition in which your research study sits (Graff and Birkenstein 2010).

An interesting tip from Larry McEnerney[5] on creating text which is persuasive is to build in a sense of instability and tension in the account of your research. Words like 'although', 'despite', 'but', 'inconsistent', 'anomaly' provide a sense of challenge and argument in the text. As with the formulation by Graff and Birkenstein, this builds on the community and body of knowledge which went before but then injects some doubt, enriching the problem and finding a solution. This creates an onward momentum which keeps the reader engaged.

Choose words carefully

A checklist of dissemination activities for Cochrane reviews includes useful advice on language use, suggesting that terms such as 'intervention' and 'outcomes' should be avoided in plain language summaries, in favour of specific terms like 'healthy living programme' and 'weight loss' (Glenton et al 2019). A really good tip is to always talk about people involved in the research – 'children' or 'overweight men' – rather than 'study participants' or (worse) 'research subjects'. We come back again to the idea of bringing the people back in to your work.

Although a general rule is to keep language simple, unusual words can sometimes be used for effect. As I was writing this section, I read a paper in a US medical journal summarising what we knew at that time from cohort studies of the rate of asymptomatic COVID-19 infection in general and particular populations (Oran and Topol 2020). I was struck by one phrase in the concluding section identifying gaps in current knowledge: 'What individual differences might account for why two persons of the same age, sex, and health status, for example, have idiosyncratic responses to SARS-CoV-2 infection? Why does one come through with nary a symptom, while the other lies near death in intensive care?'

It was the term 'nary a symptom' – a strangely colloquial and perhaps slightly archaic turn of phrase in a clear and scientific paper. But it serves its purpose, providing emphasis (compared to the flatter 'no symptoms') and perhaps even a sense of surprise and contrast. It seems like a small thing, but the choice of words matters.

There is a great book on translation by David Bellos, himself a celebrated literary translator. In an entertaining and very readable book, *Is That A Fish in Your Ear?* (Bellos 2012), he explores the nuance of meaning in the act of translation. The complexity of this act of cultural exchange cannot be over-stated. He looks for instance in how you translate a joke, noting the genius of the late translator Andrea Bell in the *Asterix* series. The skill with which she rendered style, idiom and humour – just think of the characters' names in English, from 'Getafix' to 'Dogmatix' – is unsurpassed. It is much more than word for word translation. The relevance of this is that we move from different registers or styles without thinking. We tend to speak differently to a friend or a senior colleague. We write differently in an academic paper or a postcard. But sometimes it is helpful to switch registers and to use words and language which may be slightly out of place in a different context. It may be using homely or concrete examples or analogies when writing about your research. Or playing with humour and double meanings (although this is best done sparingly). Choose your words carefully.

Be yourself – the importance of voice

One of the hardest elements to explain or define is the 'voice' in someone's writing. We know it when we see it. We could probably recognise a paragraph written by Malcolm Gladwell or Caitlin Moran without much trouble or a short extract from a documentary by Louis Theroux. The presence of the writer is partly their style and how they express themselves and partly the kinds of things that interest them. You may think that academic writing is objective and neutral and stripped of personality. But Helen Sword and others have shown that many of the best scholarly communicators bring their whole selves to the project, with all their quirks and idiosyncrasies.

A good way of practising finding your voice is by writing a blog. Sarah Chapman, knowledge broker for the UK Cochrane Centre (and former nurse), writes regular blogs, relating her personal experience to the available evidence and making sense of the research. Two of her blogs stick in my mind; her review of evidence on older people's adherence to complex medication regimens in relation to her mother with dementia and her experience of frozen shoulder. In the latter, she bookends the short piece with her story of shoulder stiffness and pain by way of memory of her grandfather, wounded in the First World War. She interrogates evidence which may be helpful, from physical therapy to electrotherapy (not much help). She then provides detailed insight from her physiotherapist, again interpreting the evidence with her own praxis or professional wisdom. There's a lot in here, but it is easy to read (Chapman 2017) www. evidentlycochrane.net/frozen-shoulder-2/.

Deborah Bowman, a professor of medical ethics, has written powerfully on the experience of being a cancer patient. This upended many of her beliefs and assumptions in her professional life, in areas like consent and patient choice:

> Throughout my treatment, my responses surprised me. I was both rational and emotional. I both wanted to know and to not know information. I was constant and changeable. Sometimes, I was taken aback by the way the arrival of a Royal Marsden envelope made me feel − like grenades on my door mat. (Bowman 2019)

It can feel exposing to use your own voice. But it can help to connect to your readers. On that note, Helen Sword devotes a chapter to the personal voice − suggesting that there is no inviolable rule that writers of academic papers cannot speak directly to their readers. She gives example of respected scholars writing as 'I', 'we' and even calling out directly to readers with 'you'. Writing in the third person – 'the author found', 'the investigators have already asserted' – is strangely distancing and formal. It removes you from your writing. Think about re-inserting your own voice and speak directly to your reader.

PRACTICAL POINTERS TO STRENGTHEN YOUR WRITING STYLE

Think about writers you like

Who do you enjoy reading – for work or in your own time? What do you like about their style? Ask your friends and colleagues to name one writer, fiction or non-fiction, who they think writes well. See if you agree. Keep a journal with reflections on your research, notes on recent books or articles which have stuck in your mind. Are there any connections between them? What is it about the themes and the way in which they were expressed that resonated with you? Take one thread, perhaps linking some disparate trends or insights from different worlds and disciplines, and try writing a short blog. Keep it personal.

Sum it up

Write a short 300-word summary of your research and try it out on your neighbour. Test how accessible it is using an online readability index, aiming for a reading age of about 13 years. Read the summary out loud. This will help you express yourself as simply and clearly as possible. Remember to start and end with the problem, why it is important and how this research adds to what we know. Why should anyone be interested? Use a brief example of individuals and families and how this research might lead to better care or experience.

Play with titles

Find three titles that you like from a few journals you read. Which papers caught your eye and how did the title contribute? You can try creating five alternative titles for your research study, testing out contrasting styles and lengths, with at least one which is boldly humorous. You can market test titles as tweets and see which versions attract the most attention – and bring in readers who stay on the page.

10

Last thoughts

This chapter sums up the thinking in this book about the need for effort and creativity in presenting and promoting research to wider audiences. In this way, the researcher acts as film director making strategic choices about content, tone and appeal for particular audiences, working closely with others. Closing thoughts include the importance of researchers making strategic choices about who, what, how and when they can best reach target groups and networks. Time is needed to do this well, including effort to convey complex findings simply. Knowing who you want to reach and where these people go is an essential component of good engagement. Researchers are asked to bring their work to life with stories and their own enthusiasms and interests. There is a moral responsibility for researchers to do what they can to get their findings used, as the world needs high-quality and reliable research at a time of information saturation and uncertainty.

Give us the pitch

I was trying to think of an appropriate metaphor to tie together the messages of this book. The use of metaphors has been a bit of a thread in the scholarly literature to describe the knowledge-practice gap, from bridges (Kazdin 2008) to translation (Straus et al 2013) to *bricolage* (Kincheloe 2001), or the craft of improvising using diverse materials to make something new. Existing metaphors are sometimes criticised (Greenhalgh and Wieringa 2011) without putting forward a concrete alternative. We like metaphors, as we like stories.

The nearest metaphor I could come up with, thinking of all the insights from the people I talked to while writing this book, was the researcher as film director. That is, you take the raw script (your research findings) but need to first of all understand your audience. Who are you trying to reach – families, young adults or older women? What makes them laugh or cry? What other films have they liked? (But don't be bound too much by what went before – who would have believed that a quirky arthouse foreign-language film about a destitute family of con artists in South Korea would be box-office gold?) How much do they know already about the context of your film, say Cold War communications, and how much do you need to tell them?

Your job then is to translate the script into a film which people will remember and enjoy. What mood do you want to create? How will you build this working with experts in lighting, cinematography, costumes and locations? What is the story arc and what is the tagline? This is the part below the title – great examples compress much of the emotion and storyline of a film into a single line, from *Double Indemnity*, 'From the moment they met, it was murder' to *Alien*, 'In space, no one can hear you scream'. How would you market it and what would be in the trailer, in terms of critical moments or findings from your study? How will it add to the body of knowledge and can you describe its place in the tradition in which it sits – 'like *Broadcast News* crossed with *His Girl Friday*'?

These are all strategic choices that you, the director, will make. But you will only bring it to life through collaboration with others. And it depends above all on your understanding and knowledge of the audience and what they want. (In fact, this metaphor does not completely work as it still assumes a passive audience rather than one which helps to shape and create a new form by working together).

How to make your research matter

Here is a recap of some of the important messages running through this book about finding ways to communicate better with a range of audiences.

Be sure your research is worth promoting

Not every research project needs active boosting and wider circulation. Some studies add usefully to a body of knowledge but in themselves do not justify active promotion. That might include some early development of a new approach, which needs further testing. Or a methodological study which may be valuable to other researchers without warranting broadsheet coverage. Given information overload, you need to understand the weight of your study and what space it should fill.

Having said that, most health and care researchers start their work because it addresses some important service gap or uncertainty. Something that perhaps has bothered them when they were practising as social workers or occupational therapists – how effective are family group conferences? What is 'good enough' in safeguarding decisions? What kinds of music therapy seem to work best for residents with dementia in care homes? Connecting back to the reasons for doing your research in the first place will help you to be a powerful advocate for the work.

In this book, I have used examples of health and care research which I think have made a difference. You will have your own personal portfolio of high-impact research in your field or area of practice. The first rule though in good engagement is understanding why the research is important and what makes it interesting and relevant to decision-makers. The best writing and communication cannot make up for a lack of passion and clarity about why the study matters in the first place. Articulating that is the first job in promoting your research.

Get to know the people you want to reach

Martin Marshall had a great turn of phrase when he asked that researchers come out of the ivory tower and engage with the 'swampy lowlands' of practice (Marshall 2014). This was in a piece arguing for more embedded forms of research, but there is a wider truth in the need for researchers to get out more and mix with people and communities they want to reach. In the present day, this could be done from the comfort of your own desk in terms of social media. Develop a presence on Twitter or Facebook, follow interesting people of influence in your target communities and listen and engage in debate where your evidence might make a useful contribution. Listening is key. Attend meetings and conferences to learn more about the context and important issues to practitioners in the field. Ask a trusted source to guide you through the networks, communities and channels and spend time if you can getting to know their values and interests.

At this time of fiscal restraints and unprecedented demands on health and care services, you will be very mindful of adding to the burden for frontline staff and decision-makers. See if you can offer something in return, perhaps providing resources that could be used in social worker learning sets or running sessions for a hospital journal club.

Many researchers in the fields of health, social care and social work started out in practice or continue to span these worlds. This hybrid position can be difficult to maintain. In a parallel field, there is an interesting body of knowledge on the role of the clinical-manager and social identity issues, for instance in allied health professions (Petchey et al 2013). There is a risk of assuming knowledge while being at some remove from frontline staff. Keep in touch with what matters to the practitioners, managers and people you are trying to reach by reading what they read and following people they follow on social media. And don't always go to the usual suspects – cast your net wide and think about the range of backgrounds and perspectives which might be relevant to your project or the populations you serve.

Engagement is the cornerstone of effective sharing of knowledge. It takes effort to build and maintain relationships with individuals and communities. But throughout this book, we have seen how researchers who invest time in meaningful engagement with the audiences they want to reach reap rewards. People share and create knowledge – every evidence journey is social.

Remember, simple is not easy

There are some good tips about writing simply and clearly from a number of people in this book. But it is difficult to do.

Researchers often do not spend enough time on the public-facing outputs, like the plain language summary. This should not be an afterthought, tacked on at the end of the study. These need careful development and testing with people who know nothing about your research. You will need several versions before you have a clear line of argument for your research, which tells the story without compromising the science. A good rule of thumb is to read out loud and test headline messages again and again with different people, including those with no connection to your study.

Practise until you find your voice

You may not know your style, but you have one. There are certain words that you use, other people's work that you cite more often, forms of writing that appeal to you. Different styles are appropriate for different audiences and purposes. But you will not be harming the integrity of your work by adding humour or making a surprise analogy with a topical issue or cultural icon. Your aim is to entertain, as well as inform. But to do this, you need to find a tone that feels authentic and true to yourself.

Be curious about the writers or thinkers you like. What appeals to you in their work? Do they have any qualities in common?

Start small with a short blog or newsletter feature and try to catch readers' attention with an interesting fact or example from your work.

This book highlights certain products or outputs which are likely to be most appropriate for particular audiences. This includes feature articles or blogs in practice journals for health and social care staff; plain language summaries for general public and those using services; and policy briefs for decision-makers at national and local level. These all need different styles and formats. Writing in different ways – from opinion pieces to formal summaries – and taking part in different events – from local radio to neighbourhood meetings – is a skill like any other. It takes time to be fluent, conversational and strike the right tone. You can work with experienced practice journal editors and intermediaries like your university communications team or outfits like theconversation.com to get better at this. But the main principle is to keep practising. It may take many drafts and iterations with others to create an output which is readable and relevant to your audience.

Make it personal – bring the people back in

A consistent thread running through this book has been the need to bring research to life with stories. This is what journalists do to connect the reader to the bigger issues at hand. You might want to use quotes or vignettes from your research or tell the story of why you did this research and its connection with you. You may have been motivated to carry out research on the hospital experience for people with learning disabilities when your autistic brother experienced poor care when having his appendix removed. You may want to start your presentation of your ethnographic study on migrants' experience of childbirth with the story of a particular Somalian woman which stuck with you. On the whole, a good rule is to use stories, not theories, to advance understanding.

Follow your curiosity

Enthusiasm is infectious. It is a good idea to follow your own interests in promoting and sharing your work. This may go beyond your particular field or discipline. For instance, like many people I have long had a geeky interest in Bletchley Park and the work that went on there. I came across a brilliant book by an organisational historian, Christopher Grey, Professor of Organisation Studies at Royal Holloway, called *Decoding Organisation* (Grey 2012). I read the whole book like a novel. Using archives and oral history, he debunks many of the myths of the lone Turing genius in a Nissan hut to describe a complex organisation, with dynamic 'tangle' of cultures and knowledge work which combined industrial-scale data analysis with high-level judgement. In doing this, he also reviews and re-shapes current organisational theories.

At the time, I was organising a seminar for health service researchers on case studies. I invited Christopher Grey who gave a great talk, bringing new perspectives of historical ethnography to our deliberations on organisational case studies in healthcare. He also of course had some killer stories from oral history work with codebreakers and analysts. My point is that I am glad I brought in a rather personal interest to my working life. Reflect on what and who interests and excites you beyond your particular study. What you bring will be particular to you, but may spark interest in others.

Be assertive – the world needs good research

I was struck by a point made in conversation with Teresa Chinn (Box 4.7), who set up a leading online nursing platform and community. She ended with a plea to researchers to do more to get their work known and not to think about this as self-promotion. From her perspective, there was too much information of dubious provenance and quality arriving in her inbox or Twitter feed. She needed to counter this with careful and robust evidence from trusted sources.

We live in an age of fake news. Not only is there much false information, but it is better at reaching people than information which is true. Researchers at MIT used different analytic methods to review ten years' worth of Twitter data and concluded that 'falsehood diffused significantly farther, faster, deeper, and more broadly than the truth in all categories of information' (Vosoughi et al 2018).

What this means is that researchers have a responsibility to share good evidence. It is part of the role of the 'engaged scholar' (Van de Ven 2007) – the moral or civic duty for researchers to engage in public conversations and debate, on Twitter and through relevant community groups. This marks the convergence of trends, from open science, underlining the democratic rights to sharing research findings and data in a timely and accessible way, to longstanding debates on the role and responsibility of public and social intellectuals (Chapman and Greenhow 2019).

This responsibility includes reaching people with clear messages, while being true to the science. This means not over-claiming for single studies and presenting findings with attention to the weight and levels of certainty which the study design and findings allow. Incidents of actual deception in research are rare. But we are collectively haunted by those cases we know about. This includes the social psychologist, Diedrik Stapel, found guilty of scientific fraud in studies of human attitudes and behaviour who stated: 'I wanted to manipulate the truth and make the world just a little more beautiful than it is.'[1] There is a temptation for us all to smooth off the edges and simplify for effect. But there is a reasonable path between clarity and accuracy, which many researchers tread well.

Researchers start their work wanting to make a difference. The extra steps and actions set out in this book and elsewhere to reach and engage people in meaningful ways, paying attention to story, language and appropriate channels are part of the job of a researcher in the 21st century. Research findings should not stay in the library or on the university bookshelf. They should be translated and worked up with the right communities into new policies, decisions, conversations and practice. This is not a one-off event, but a social process with multiple interactions and exchanges. Understanding who you are trying to reach and the best ways to reach them is a core part of your mission. Practising different ways of communicating and testing these out with your target audience will strengthen your outputs. You are the best person to do this, working closely with others. Now you need to get your research out into the world.

Notes

Chapter 1

[1] McDonald (2015) provides a great general account of Nightingale's work as a social scientist and reformer, in areas from hospital management to workhouse infirmaries through to rural health and agrarian reform in India.

Chapter 3

[1] Using panels of clinicians (initially physicians, but now includes nurses and rehabilitation therapists) to assess evidence for relevance and newsworthiness, as described here: http://hiru.mcmaster.ca/more/

Chapter 4

[1] JLA Adult Social Work Top 10 (2008) www.jla.nihr.ac.uk/priority-setting-partnerships/adult-social-work/top-10-priorities.htm

[2] Throughout this chapter, I mention many web-based reviews of NIHR research, engaging practitioners and other stakeholders to create a narrative on topics from assistive technology to ward staffing. These can be accessed at https://evidence.nihr.ac.uk/themed-reviews/

[3] Although it is not possible to measure precisely rates of research use by practitioners, studies cited by Renolen et al (2018) of clinical nurses' self-reported behaviour show infrequent use of new scientific knowledge.

[4] For a more detailed account of the theoretical ways in which networks generate and mobilise research, see Greenhalgh 2018: 182–202.

Chapter 5

[1] For more information, see www.jla.nihr.ac.uk/about-the-james-lind-alliance/

Chapter 6

[1] It is worth also checking out the series of very readable blogs by Paul Cairney on all aspects of policymaking and evidence use, from COVID-19 to environmental issues at https://paulcairney.wordpress.com/

[2] www.gov.uk/guidance/what-works-network

Chapter 7

[1] https://parliamentlive.tv/Event/Index/8437ac8b-626a-4213-9433-1c28559c477d House of Commons Health Committee 9 May 2016. As an

aside, the televised session is well worth watching, as a masterclass in forensic evidence-based grilling by an MP who was formerly a breast surgeon.

Chapter 8

1. www.youtube.com/watch?v=cXJJvvjSB9c
2. In a nicely participative mode, Jon Sutton shared his thoughts on telling stories in psychology and effective writing as a Google Doc which people have contributed to and strengthened https://docs.google.com/document/d/1IysRCrrJgPkI3Or_p-6m3Fc1o0WoZYZQZWgHVGZlU7Y/edit?ts=5e7226f9
3. www.walesonline.co.uk/news/health/airline-pilot-vowed-improve-nhs-1915281
4. This can now be accessed free online www.scientificadvertising.com/ScientificAdvertising.pdf
5. Larry McEnerney (Lecture 26 June 2014) www.youtube.com/watch?v=vtIzMaLkCaM (accessed 1 March 2021)
6. Lamont, T. (2020) 'Learning from social sciences at a time of crisis', 24 April, *BMJ Opinion* https://blogs.bmj.com/bmj/2020/04/24/tara-lamont-learning-from-social-sciences-at-a-time-of-crisis/

Chapter 9

1. Often attributed to Einstein, but may be an elegant compression of his thoughts in a lecture, as noted by Robinson (2018) in *Nature*. Robinson, A. 2018. Did Einstein really say that?. *Nature*, 557(7703): 30–1.
2. NIHR (2018), doi: 10.3310/signal-00578
3. NIHR (2018), doi: 10.3310/signal-000542
4. I was alerted to this example on Twitter by David Nunan @dnunan79 of the Oxford Centre for Evidence Based Medicine, who works in research on physical activity and nutrition and is alert to issues of exaggeration and spin on social media and elsewhere.
5. Larry McEnerney (Lecture 26 June 2014) www.youtube.com/watch?v=vtIzMaLkCaM (accessed 1 March 2021).

Chapter 10

1. Alerted to this quote by Jon Sutton – see Chapter 8, endnote 2 – from *De Volkskrant* on 31 October 2011.

Further reading

I have selected resources which I have found particularly helpful on the theory and practice of evidence use, with a brief description of what they add. These are focused on fairly recent publications, but provide links back to some of the seminal early work in this field. I have not included here some of the individual research studies tracking how knowledge influences policy and practice referenced in this book. Many of these are NIHR funded and can be accessed in full (free) from www.journalslibrary.nihr.ac.uk.

On how evidence is used in policy and practice (with particular reference to health and care)

Boaz, A., Davies, H., Fraser, A. and Nutley, S. (eds) (2019) *What Works Now? Evidence-informed Policy and Practice*, Bristol: Policy Press. (Useful and current academic account of activity to embed evidence in public services, with a focus on the UK including initiatives such as the What Works Centres – with analysis across local government, criminal justice, education and international development as well as health and a broad focus on academic social sciences.)

Greenhalgh, T. (2018) *How to Implement Evidence-based Healthcare*, Oxford: Wiley Blackwell. (Combination of theoretical handbook on embedding evidence, from behaviour change to complexity theory, and practical frameworks and tools for practitioners and organisations wanting to use evidence to drive improvements, with many worked examples from the author's research and clinical practice.)

Cairney, P. (2016) *The Politics of Evidence-based Policymaking*, London: Palgrave Macmillan. (Authoritative account of how policymakers handle ambiguity and use evidence, with worked examples in areas like tobacco control and environment, through the lens of public policy theory.)

Langer L., Tripney, J. and Gough, D.A. (2016) *The Science of Using Science: Researching the Use of Research Evidence in Decision-Making*, London: EPPI-Centre, Social Science Research Unit, UCL Institute of Education, University College London, https:// eppi.ioe.ac.uk/cms/Default.aspx?tabid=3504. (Comprehensive review of evidence on approaches to research use, including scoping of wider sources from social marketing to adult learning theory.)

Breckon, J. and Dodson, J. (2016) *Alliance for Useful Evidence. Using Research Evidence: A Practice Guide*, NESTA, www. alliance4usefulevidence.org/assets/Using-Research-Evidence-for-Success-A-Practice-Guide-v6-web.pdf. (Useful practical guide for decision-makers in government and service leaders on making better use of evidence and judging strength, quality and relevance with examples from range of public policy. Draws on Langer review – see earlier reference.)

Davies, H.T.O., Powell, A.E. and Nutley, S.M. (2015) 'Mobilising knowledge to improve UK health care: learning from other countries and other sectors – a multimethod mapping study', *Health Services and Delivery Research*, 3(27), www. journalslibrary.nihr.ac.uk/hsdr/hsdr03270#/full-report. (This includes a useful conceptual mapping of evidence on knowledge use, as well as new learning from a range of international research agencies on their activities and approaches.)

Straus, S., Tetroe, J. and Graham, I.D. (2013) *Knowledge Translation in Health Care: Moving from Evidence to Practice*, Chichester: John Wiley & Sons. (Comprehensive international academic account of theoretical and empirical evidence on knowledge mobilisation in health and healthcare, from synthesising evidence to audit and feedback interventions.)

The Milbank Quarterly, Virtual Issue (2011) 'Facilitating the use of research evidence', Wiley Online Library. (This contains links to over 20 key papers on the topic from thought leaders in the field, including John Lavis, Jonathan Lomas, Kieran Walshe, Trish Greenhalgh, Jacqueline Tetroe and others.)

Nutley, S., Walter, I. and Davies, H.T.O. (2007) *Using Evidence: How Research Can Inform Public Services*, Bristol: Policy Press. (Useful primer of theory and research on use of evidence by decision-makers in fields from criminal justice to social care.)

On research impact

Dunleavy, P. and Tinkler, J. (2020) *Maximizing the Impacts of Academic Research: How to Grow the Recognition, Influence, Practical Application and Public Understanding of Science and Scholarship*, London: Macmillan. (Comprehensive overview on academic outputs, from writing a journal article to optimising citation counts as well as a section on writing for public audiences. Draws on their work for the LSE Impact of Social Sciences blog – see LSE reference.)

Smith, K.E., Bandola-Gill, J., Meer, N., Stewart, E. and Watermeyer, R. (2020) *The Impact Agenda: Controversies, Consequences and Challenges*, Bristol: Policy Press. (Critical review and scholarly debate on the way in which research impact is measured and understood across various fields and disciplines.)

Reed, M. (2018) *The Research Impact Handbook* (2nd edn), Fast Track Impact. (Very readable primer on all aspects of creating research impact for academics wanting to make a difference, with detailed advice on areas like intellectual property and writing impact case studies. Draws on his own experience as an academic in agrifood with useful case studies and practical examples.)

LSE Impact of Social Sciences blog, https://blogs.lse.ac.uk/impactofsocialsciences/. (This is a useful hub for a series of blogs from leading thinkers and researchers on theory and practice of impact, from guide to altmetrics to writing style. This resource was started in September 2011, but is still active with new content for researchers posted regularly.)

On language, style and writing

There are many style guides – from classics like George Orwell's rules for writers in his 1946 essay 'Politics and the English Language' (www.orwell.ru/library/essays/politics/english/e_polit/) to Strunk and White's 'Elements of Style' in 1959, London: The MacMillan Press (adapted from an earlier manual). There are useful reference guides for journalists and writers from *The Economist* (Wroe, A. (2018) *The Economist Style Guide*, London: Profile Books), *The Guardian* (www.theguardian.com/guardian-observer-style-guide-c) and other newspapers on usage and preferred terms in modern English. For researchers, there is useful guidance from Patrick Dunleavy on good academic writing at https://blogs.lse.ac.uk/writingforresearch/ with advice from storyboarding your research to writing blogs. Similar wise counsel is provided by Rachel Cayley in her blog series https://explorationsofstyle.com – I particularly enjoyed her post on using writing to clarify thinking.

Sword, H. (2012) *Stylish Academic Writing*, Cambridge, Mass: Harvard University Press. (I draw on the work of Helen Sword in Chapter 9 on use of language and would recommend reading her book in full, for entertainment as well as instruction. A good blog summarising her work and argument is set out in https://blogs.lse.ac.uk/impactofsocialsciences/2012/05/14/stylish-academic-writing/)

On dissemination and engagement

Other useful free manuals and guides on topics from writing impact case studies to dissemination plans include:

Glenton, C., Rosenbaum, S. and Fønhus, M.S. (2019) *Checklist and Guidance for Disseminating Findings from Cochrane Intervention Reviews*, https://training.cochrane.org/online-learning/knowledge-translation/how-share-cochraneevidence/dissemination-essentials-checklist. (Useful worked examples on how to maximise research findings, including presenting numerical findings in reliable and accessible ways, focused mainly on systematic reviews.)

Tilley, H., Ball, L. and Cassidy, C. (2018) *REF Impact Toolkit. Overseas Development Institute*, www.odi.org/publications/11089-research-excellence-framework-ref-impact-toolkit. (Six modules with helpful step-by-step advice on setting out pathways to impact and develop case studies.)

ESRC impact toolkit, https://esrc.ukri.org/research/impact-toolkit/. (Various online resources on wide range of areas, from communication and impact strategies to logic models for demonstrating impact.)

Health Canada (2017) *Knowledge Translation Planner*, www.canada.ca/content/dam/hc-sc/documents/corporate/about-healthcanada/reports-publications/grants-contributions/KT%20Planner-EN-2017-10-16.pdf. (Step-by-step guide to project planning for impact.)

Health Foundation (2017) *Communicating Your Research: A Toolkit*, www.health.org.uk/publications/communicating-your-research-a-toolkit. (Helpful guide on communications planning, including targeting particular channels.)

Glenton, C. (2017) *How To Write a Plain Language Summary of a Cochrane Intervention Review*, Cochrane Norway, www.cochrane.no/sites/cochrane.no/files/public/uploads/how_to_write_a_cochrane_ pls_12th_february_2019.pdf. (Useful step-by-step guide on writing a plain language summary, although focused on systematic reviews.)

References

Adams, C.E., Jayaram, M., Bodart, A.Y.M., Sampson, S., Zhao, S. and Montgomery, A.A. (2016) 'Tweeting links to Cochrane Schizophrenia Group reviews: a randomised controlled trial', *BMJ Open*, 6(3): e010509.

Adams, R.C., Challenger, A., Bratton, L., Boivin, J., Bott, L., Powell, G., Williams, A., Chambers, C.D. and Sumner, P. (2019) 'Claims of causality in health news: a randomised trial', *BMC Medicine*, 17(1): 1–11.

Aiken, L.H., Sloane, D.M., Bruyneel, L., Van den Heede, K., Griffiths, P., Busse, R. et al (2014) 'Nurse staffing and education and hospital mortality in nine European countries: a retrospective observational study', *The Lancet*, 383: 1824–30.

Alvesson, M., Gabriel, Y. and Paulsen, R. (2017) *Return to Meaning: A Social Science with Something to Say*, Oxford: Oxford University Press.

Appleby, J., Raleigh, V., Frosini, F., Bevan, G., Gao, H. and Lyscom, T. (2011) *Variations in Health Care: The Good, the Bad and the Inexplicable*, London: King's Fund.

Atkins, L., Smith, J.A., Kelly, M.P. and Michie, S. (2013) 'The process of developing evidence-based guidance in medicine and public health: a qualitative study of views from the inside', *Implementation Science*, 8(1): 1–12.

Badenoch, D. and Tomlin, A. (2015) 'Keeping up to date with reliable mental health research: Minervation White Paper'. Available from: www.minervation.com (accessed 19 October 2020).

Banks, S., Herrington, T. and Carter, K. (2017) 'Pathways to co-impact: action research and community organising', *Educational Action Research*, 25(4): 541–59.

Bath, P.M., Woodhouse, L.J., Appleton, J.P., Beridze, M., Christensen, H., Dineen, R.A. et al (2017) 'Antiplatelet therapy with aspirin, clopidogrel, and dipyridamole versus clopidogrel alone or aspirin and dipyridamole in patients with acute cerebral ischaemia (TARDIS): a randomised, open-label, phase 3 superiority trial', *The Lancet*, 391(10123): 850–9.

Baxter, K., Heavey, E. and Birks, Y. (2020) 'Choice and control in social care: experiences of older self-funders in England', *Social Policy & Administration*, 54(3): 460–74.

Bayley, J. and Phipps, D. (2019) 'Extending the concept of research impact literacy: levels of literacy, institutional role and ethical considerations', *Emerald Open Research*, 1: 14.

Bellos, D. (2012) *Is That a Fish in Your Ear? Translation and the Meaning of Everything*, London: Penguin Books.

Beresford, P. (2016) *All Our Welfare: Towards Participatory Social Policy*, Bristol: Policy Press.

Best, A. and Holmes, B. (2010) 'Systems thinking, knowledge and action: towards better models and methods', *Evidence & Policy: A Journal of Research, Debate and Practice*, 6(2): 145–59.

Bickerdike, L., Booth, A., Wilson, P.M., Farley, K. and Wright, K. (2017) 'Social prescribing: less rhetoric and more reality. A systematic review of the evidence', *BMJ Open*, 7(4): e013384.

Boaz, A. and Nutley, S. (2019) 'Using evidence', in A. Boaz, H. Davies, A. Fraser and S. Nutley (eds) *What Works Now? Evidence-Informed Policy and Practice*, Bristol: Policy Press, pp 251–77.

Boaz, A., Biri, D. and McKevitt, C. (2016) 'Rethinking the relationship between science and society: has there been a shift in attitudes to patient and public involvement and public engagement in science in the United Kingdom?', *Health Expectations*, 19(3): 592–601.

Boaz, A., Hanney, S., Borst, R., O'Shea, A. and Kok, M. (2018) 'How to engage stakeholders in research: design principles to support improvement', *Health Research Policy and Systems*, 16(1): 1–9.

Boaz, A., Davies, H., Fraser, A. and Nutley, S. (eds) (2019) *What Works Now? Evidence-informed Policy and Practice*, Bristol: Policy Press.

Bornbaum, C.C., Kornas, K., Peirson, L. and Rosella, L.C. (2015) 'Exploring the function and effectiveness of knowledge brokers as facilitators of knowledge translation in health-related settings: a systematic review and thematic analysis', *Implementation Science*, 10: 1–12.

Bowman, D. (2019) 'I'm a Professor of Medical Ethics, but having cancer changed my beliefs about medicine'. Available from: www.royalmarsden.nhs.uk/im-professor-medical-ethics-having-cancer-changed-my-beliefs-about-medicine (accessed 24 October 2020).

Boyd, B. (2009) *On the Origin of Stories: Evolution, Cognition, and Fiction*, Cambridge, Mass: Harvard University Press.

Braithwaite, J., Glasziou, P. and Westbrook, J. (2020) 'The three numbers you need to know about healthcare: the 60–30–10 challenge', *BMC Medicine*, 18: 1–8.

Breckon, J. and Gough, D. (2019) 'Using evidence in the UK', in A. Boaz, H. Davies, A. Fraser and S. Nutley (eds) *What Works Now? Evidence-Informed Policy and Practice*, Bristol: Policy Press, pp 285–302.

Brooks, P. (1984) *Reading for the Plot: Design and Intention in Narrative*, New York: AA Knopf.

Brown, J.S. and Duguid, P. (2017) *The Social Life of Information: Updated, with a New Preface*, Boston, Mass: Harvard Business Review Press.

Cairney, P. (2016) *The Politics of Evidence-Based Policymaking*, London: Palgrave Macmillan.

Cairney, P. (2020) *Understanding Public Policy* (2nd edn), London: Red Globe Press.

Cairney, P. and Kwiatkowski, R. (2017) 'How to communicate effectively with policymakers: combine insights from psychology and policy studies', *Palgrave Communications*, 3(1): 1–8.

Campbell, J. (2008) *The Hero with a Thousand Faces* (3rd edn), Novato, Calif: New World Library.

Carroll, N. and Conboy, K. (2020) 'Normalising the "new normal": changing tech-driven work practices under pandemic time pressure', *International Journal of Information Management*, 55: 102186.

Chakravarthy, U., Harding, S.P., Rogers, C.A., Downes, S.M., Lotery, A.J., Culliford, L.A. et al (2013) 'Alternative treatments to inhibit VEGF in age-related choroidal neovascularisation: 2-year findings of the IVAN randomised controlled trial', *The Lancet*, 382 (9900): 1258–67.

Chalmers, I. and Glasziou, P. (2009) 'Avoidable waste in the production and reporting of research evidence', *The Lancet*, 374(9683): 86–9.

Chapman, A.L. and Greenhow, C. (2019) 'Citizen-scholars: social media and the changing nature of scholarship', *Publications*, 7(1): 11.

Chapman, S. (2017) 'Frozen shoulder: making choices about treatment', 12 October. Available from: www.evidentlycochrane.net/frozen-shoulder-2/ (accessed 24 October 2020).

Charon, R. (2008) *Narrative Medicine: Honoring the Stories of Illness*, Oxford: Oxford University Press.

Christensen, C.M. (2013) *The Innovator's Dilemma: When New Technologies Cause Great Firms to Fail*, Boston, Mass: Harvard Business Review Press.

Clark, D.M. (2018) 'Realizing the mass public benefit of evidence-based psychological therapies: the IAPT program', *Annual Review of Clinical Psychology*, 14: 159–83.

Cook, E. (1913) *The Life of Florence Nightingale Vol 2 (1862–1910)*, London: Macmillan, pp 25–35. Available as ebook (2012), Urbana Illinois: Project Gutenberg, at http://www.gutenberg.org/files/40058/40058-h/40058-h.htm (accessed 22 March 2021).

Correll, C.U., Galling, B., Pawar, A., Krivko, A., Bonetto, C., Ruggeri, M. et al (2018) 'Comparison of early intervention services vs treatment as usual for early-phase psychosis: a systematic review, meta-analysis, and meta-regression', *JAMA Psychiatry*, 75: 555–65.

Cowan, K. and Oliver, S. (2021) *The James Lind Alliance Guidebook* (Version 10), Southampton: National Institute for Health Research Evaluation, Trials and Studies Coordinating Centre. Available from: www.jla.nihr.ac.uk/jla-guidebook/ (accessed 13 March 2021).

Currie, G., Waring, J. and Finn, R. (2008) 'The limits of knowledge management for UK public services modernization: the case of patient safety and service quality', *Public Administration*, 86(2): 363–85.

Davies, H.T.O., Powell, A.E. and Nutley, S.M. (2015) 'Mobilising knowledge to improve UK health care: learning from other countries and other sectors – a multimethod mapping study', *Health Services & Delivery Research*, 3(27), https://doi.org/10.3310/hsdr03270

Dixon-Woods, M. (2014) 'The problem of context in quality improvement', *Perspectives on Context: A Selection of Essays Considering the Role of Context in Successful Quality Improvement*, Health Foundation. Available from: www.health.org.uk/publications/perspectives-on-context (accessed 14 March 2021).

Dopson, S., Bennett, C., Fitzgerald, L., Ferlie, E., Fischer, M., Ledger, J., McCulloch, J. and McGivern, G. (2013) 'Health care managers' access and use of management research', NIHR Service Delivery and Organisation Programme.

Drummond, M. and Banta, D. (2009) 'Health technology assessment in the United Kingdom', *International Journal of Technology Assessment in Health Care*, 25(S1): 178–81.

Dunleavy, P. and Tinkler, J. (2020) *Maximizing the Impacts of Academic Research: How to Grow the Recognition, Influence, Practical Application and Public Understanding of Science and Scholarship*, London: Macmillan.

DuVal, G. and Shah, S. (2020) 'When does evidence from clinical trials influence health policy? A qualitative study of officials in nine African countries of the factors behind the HIV policy decision to adopt Option B+', *Evidence & Policy: A Journal of Research, Debate and Practice*, 16(1): 123–44.

Elbow, P. (2013) 'Maybe academics aren't so stupid after all', *OUPblog*, 6 February. Available from: https://blog.oup.com/2013/02/academic-speech-patterns-linguistics/ (accessed 20 October 2020).

Elliott, J.H., Turner, T., Clavisi, O., Thomas, J., Higgins, J.P., Mavergames, C. and Gruen, R.L. (2014) 'Living systematic reviews: an emerging opportunity to narrow the evidence-practice gap', *PLOS Medicine*, 11(2): e1001603.

Engebretsen, M. and Kennedy, H. (eds) (2020) *Data Visualization in Society*, Amsterdam: Amsterdam University Press.

Evans, S. and Scarbrough, H. (2014) 'Supporting knowledge translation through collaborative translational research initiatives: "bridging" versus "blurring" boundary-spanning approaches in the UK CLAHRC initiative', *Social Science & Medicine*, 106: 119–27.

Fanshawe, T.R., Halliwell, W., Lindson, N., Aveyard, P., Livingstone-Banks, J. and Hartmann-Boyce, J. (2017) 'Tobacco cessation interventions for young people', *Cochrane Database of Systematic Reviews*, 11: CD003289.

Featherstone, K., Northcott, A., Harden, J., Harrison-Denning, K., Tope, R., Bale, S. and Bridges, J. (2019) 'Refusal and resistance to care by people living with dementia being cared for within acute hospital wards: an ethnographic study', *Health Services & Delivery Research*, 7(11), https://doi.org/10.3310/hsdr07110

Franck, G. (2019) 'The economy of attention', *Journal of Sociology*, 55(1): 8–19.

Freeman, R. (2007) 'Epistemological bricolage: how practitioners make sense of learning', *Administration & Society*, 39(4): 476–96.

Fulop, N.J., Ramsay, A.I.G., Hunter, R.M., McKevitt, C., Perry, C., Turner, S.J. et al (2019) 'Evaluation of reconfigurations of acute stroke services in different regions of England and lessons for implementation: a mixed-methods study', *Health Services and Delivery Research*, 7(7), https://doi.org/10.3310/hsdr07070

Gabbay, J. and le May, A. (2011) *Practice-based Evidence for Health Care: Clinical Mindlines*, Abingdon: Routledge.

Gates, S., Lall, R., Quinn, T., Deakin, C.D., Cooke, M.W., Horton, J., Lamb, S.E., Slowther, A.M., Woollard, M., Carson, A. and Smyth, M. (2017) 'Prehospital randomised assessment of a mechanical compression device in out-of-hospital cardiac arrest (PARAMEDIC): a pragmatic, cluster randomised trial and economic evaluation', *Health Technology Assessment*, 21(11), https://doi.org/10.3310/hta21110

Gawande, A. (2014) *Being Mortal: Medicine and What Matters in the End*, New York: Metropolitan Books.

Glasziou, P. and Chalmers, I. (2018) 'Research waste is still a scandal: an essay by Paul Glasziou and Iain Chalmers', *BMJ*, 363: k4645.

Glenton, C. (2017) 'How to write a plain language summary of a Cochrane intervention review', Cochrane Norway. Available from: www.cochrane.no/sites/cochrane.no/files/public/uploads/how_to_write_a_cochrane_pls_12th_february_2019.pdf (accessed 26 February 2021).

Glenton, C., Rosenbaum, S. and Fønhus, M.S. (2019) 'Checklist and guidance for disseminating findings from Cochrane intervention reviews' Cochrane. Available from: https://training.cochrane.org/sites/training.cochrane.org/files/public/uploads/Checklist%20FINAL%20version%201.1%20April%20 2020pdf.pdf (accessed 26 February 2021).

Gough, D., Maidment, C. and Sharples, J. (2018) *UK What Works Centres: Aims, Methods and Contexts*, London: EPPI-Centre. Available from: https://eppi.ioe.ac.uk/cms/Default.aspx?tabid=3731 (accessed 14 March 2021).

Graff, G. and Birkenstein, C. (2010) *'They Say/I Say': The Moves that Matter in Persuasive Writing* (2nd edn), New York: Norton.

Graham, I.D. and Tetroe, J. (2007) 'Some theoretical underpinnings of knowledge translation', *Academy of Emergency Medicine*, 14(11): 936–41.

Gravier, E. (2019) 'Spending 2 hours in nature each week can make you happier and healthier, new study says', 2 July, cnbc.com (online), www.cnbc.com/2019/07/02/spending-2-hours-in-nature-per-week-can-make-you-happier-and-healthier.html (accessed 14 March 2021).

Green, L.W. (2008) 'Making research relevant: if it is an evidence-based practice, where's the practice-based evidence?' *Family Practice*, 25(Suppl 1): i20–4.

Greenhalgh, T. (2018) *How to Implement Evidence-Based Healthcare*, Oxford: Wiley Blackwell.

Greenhalgh, T. and Wieringa, S. (2011) 'Is it time to drop the "knowledge translation" metaphor? A critical literature review', *Journal of the Royal Society of Medicine*, 104(12): 501–09.

Greenhalgh, T. and Fahy, N. (2015) 'Research impact in the community-based health sciences: an analysis of 162 case studies from the 2014 UK Research Excellence Framework', *BMC Medicine*, 13(1): 1–12.

Greenhalgh, T., Schmid, M.B., Czypionka, T., Bassler, D. and Gruer, L. (2020) 'Face masks for the public during the covid-19 crisis', *BMJ*, 369: m1435.

Grey, C. (2012) *Decoding Organization: Bletchley Park, Codebreaking and Organization Studies*, Cambridge: Cambridge University Press.

Griffiths, P., Ball, J., Bloor, K., Böhning, D., Briggs, J., Dall'Ora, C. et al (2018) 'Nurse staffing levels, missed vital signs and mortality in hospitals: retrospective longitudinal observational study', *Health Services & Delivery Research*: 6(38), https://doi.org/10.3310/hsdr06380

Hanney, S.R., Castle-Clarke, S., Grant, J., Guthrie, S., Henshall, C., Mestre-Ferrandiz, J., Pistollato, M., Pollitt, A., Sussex, J. and Wooding, S. (2015) 'How long does biomedical research take? Studying the time taken between biomedical and health research and its translation into products, policy, and practice', *Health Research Policy and Systems*, 13(1): 1–18.

Harris, R., Sims, S., Leamy, M., Levenson, R., Davies, N., Brearley, S. et al (2019) 'Intentional rounding in hospital wards to improve regular interaction and engagement between nurses and patients: a realist evaluation', *Health Services & Delivery Research*, 7(35), https://doi.org/10.3310/hsdr07350

Haux, T. (2019) *Dimensions of Impact in the Social Sciences: The Case of Social Policy, Sociology and Political Science Research*, Bristol: Policy Press.

Hickey, G., Richards, T. and Sheehy, J. (2018) 'Co-production from proposal to paper', *Nature*, 562: 29–31.

Hogwood, B.W. and Gunn, L.A. (1984) *Policy Analysis for the Real World*, Oxford: Oxford University Press.

Holmes, A., Dixon-Woods, M., Ahmad, R., Brewster, E., Castro Sanchez, E.M., Secci, F., Zingg, W. et al (2015) *Infection Prevention and Control: Lessons from Acute Care in England. Towards a Whole Health Economy Approach*, Health Foundation. Available from: www.health.org.uk/publications/infection-prevention-and-control-lessons-from-acute-care-in-england (accessed 14 March 2021).

Holmes, B.J., Best, A., Davies, H., Hunter, D., Kelly, M.P., Marshall, M. and Rycroft-Malone, J. (2017) 'Mobilising knowledge in complex health systems: a call to action', *Evidence & Policy*, 13(3): 539–60.

Hook, D.W., Calvert, I. and Hahnel, M. (2019) *The Ascent of Open Access: An Analysis of the Open Access Landscape since the Turn of the Millennium*. Available from: https://digitalscience. figshare.com/articles/report/The_Ascent_of_Open_Access/ 7618751 (accessed 14 March 2021).

Hopkins, C. (1923) *Scientific Advertising*, New York: Crown Publishers.

Houghton, C., Meskell, P., Delaney, H., Smalle, M., Glenton, C., Booth, A. et al (2020) 'Barriers and facilitators to healthcare workers' adherence with infection prevention and control (IPC) guidelines for respiratory infectious diseases: a rapid qualitative evidence synthesis', *Cochrane Database of Systematic Reviews*, 4.

Hutchinson, J.R. and Huberman, M. (1994) 'Knowledge dissemination and use in science and mathematics education: a literature review', *Journal of Science Education and Technology*, 3: 27–47.

Isett, K.R. and Hicks, D. (2020) 'Pathways from research into public decision making: intermediaries as the third community', *Perspectives on Public Management and Governance*, 3(1): 45–58.

Johnson, D., Deterding, S., Kuhn, K.A., Staneva, A., Stoyanov, S. and Hides, L. (2016) 'Gamification for health and wellbeing: a systematic review of the literature', *Internet Interventions*, 6: 89–106.

Kam, C.D. (2005) 'Who toes the party line? Cues, values, and individual differences', *Political Behavior*, 27(2): 163–82.

Kazdin, A. E. (2008) 'Evidence-based treatment and practice: new opportunities to bridge clinical research and practice, enhance the knowledge base, and improve patient care', *American Psychologist*, 63(3), 146–59.

Kincheloe, J.L. (2001) 'Describing the bricolage: conceptualizing a new rigor in qualitative research', *Qualitative Inquiry*, 7(6): 679–92.

Kingdon, J. (1995) *Agendas, Alternatives and Public Policies* (2nd edn), New York: Harper Collins.

Lamont, T. (2020) 'But does it work? Evidence, policy-making and systems thinking: comment on "what can policy-makers get out of systems thinking? Policy partners' experiences of a systems-focused research collaboration in preventive health"', *International Journal of Health Policy and Management*, 10(5): 287–9, doi: 10.34172/ijhpm.2020.71

Landhuis, E. (2016) 'Scientific literature: information overload', *Nature*, 535: 457–8.

Langer, L., Tripney, J. and Gough, D.A. (2016) *The Science of Using Science: Researching the Use of Research Evidence in Decision-Making*, London: EPPI-Centre, Social Science Research Unit, UCL Institute of Education, University College London. Available from: https://eppi.ioe.ac.uk/cms/Default. aspx?tabid=3504 (accessed 14 March 2021).

Larivière, V., Gingras, Y. and Archambault, É. (2009) 'The decline in the concentration of citations, 1900–2007', *Journal of the American Society for Information Science and Technology*, 60(4): 858–62.

Lave, J. and Wenger, E. (1991) *Situated Learning: Legitimate Peripheral Participation*, New York: Cambridge University Press.

Lavis, J.N., Permanand, G., Oxman, A.D., Lewin, S. and Fretheim, A. (2009) SUPPORT Tools for evidence-informed health policymaking (STP) 13: preparing and using policy briefs to support evidence-informed policymaking. *Health Research Policy and Systems*, 7(Suppl 1): S13, doi:10.1186/1478-4505-7-S1-S13

Layard, R., Clark, D.M., Knapp, M. and Mayraz, G. (2007) 'Cost-benefit analysis of psychological therapy', *National Institute Economic Review*, 202(1): 90–8.

Leder, D. (1990) *The Absent Body*, Chicago: University of Chicago Press.

Leith, S. (2012) *You Talkin' to Me: Rhetoric from Aristotle to Obama*, London: Profile Books.

Lindstrom, M. (2012) *Brandwashed: Tricks Companies Use to Manipulate our Minds and Persuade Us to Buy*, London: Kogan Page Publishers.

Lomas, J. (2000) 'Using "linkage and exchange" to move research into policy at a Canadian foundation', *Health Affairs (Millwood)*, 19(3): 236–40.

Maben, J., Peccei, R., Adams, M., Robert, G., Richardson, A., Murrells, T. and Morrow, E. (2012) *Exploring the Relationship between Patients' Experiences of Care and the Influence of Staff Motivation, Affect and Wellbeing*, Final report. Southampton: NIHR service delivery and organization programme.

Maguire, L.K. and Clarke, M. (2014) 'How much do you need: a randomised experiment of whether readers can understand the key messages from summaries of Cochrane Reviews without reading the full review', *Journal of the Royal Society of Medicine*, 107(11): 444–9.

Marshall, M.N. (2014) 'Bridging the ivory towers and the swampy lowlands: increasing the impact of health services research on quality improvement', *International Journal for Quality in Health Care*, 26(1): 1–5.

May, C.R. and Finch, T. (2009) 'Implementing, embedding, and integrating practices: an outline of normalization process theory', *Sociology*, 43(3): 535–54.

May, C.R., Eton, D.T., Boehmer, K., Gallacher, K., Hunt, K., MacDonald, S. et al (2014) 'Rethinking the patient: using Burden of Treatment Theory to understand the changing dynamics of illness', *BMC Health Services Research*, 14(1): 1–11.

Maybin, J. (2016) *Producing Health Policy: Knowledge and Knowing in Government Policy Work*, Basingstoke: Palgrave Macmillan.

McDonald, L. (ed) (2005) *Collected Works of Florence Nightingale* (Vol. 8), Waterloo ON: Wilfrid Laurier University Press.

McDonald, L. (2015) 'Florence Nightingale: a research-based approach to health, healthcare and hospital safety', in F. Collyer (ed) *The Palgrave Handbook of Social Theory in Health, Illness and Medicine*, New York: Springer, pp 59–74.

Meacock, R., Anselmi, L., Kristensen, S.R., Doran, T. and Sutton, M. (2017) 'Higher mortality rates amongst emergency patients admitted to hospital at weekends reflect a lower probability of admission', *Journal of Health Services Research & Policy*, 22(1): 12–19.

Mintrom, M. (2019) 'So you want to be a policy entrepreneur?', *Policy Design and Practice*, 2(4): 307–23.

Mir, G., Salway, S., Kai, J., Karlsen, S., Bhopal, R., Ellison, G.T. and Sheikh, A. (2013) 'Principles for research on ethnicity and health: the Leeds Consensus Statement', *The European Journal of Public Health*, 23(3): 504–10.

Mitchell, K.R., Purcell, C., Forsyth, R., Barry, S., Hunter, R., Simpson, S.A. et al (2020) 'A peer-led intervention to promote sexual health in secondary schools: the STASH feasibility study', *Public Health Research*, 8(15), https://doi.org/10.3310/phr08150

Moat, K.A., Lavis, J.N. and Abelson, J. (2013) 'How contexts and issues influence the use of policy-relevant research syntheses: a critical interpretive synthesis', *The Milbank Quarterly*, 91(3): 604–48.

Morris, S., Hunter, R.M., Ramsay, A.I.G., Boaden, R., McKevitt, C., Perry, C. et al (2014) 'Impact of centralising acute stroke services in English metropolitan areas on mortality and length of hospital stay: difference-in-differences analysis', *BMJ*, 349: g4757.

Morris, S., Ramsay, A.I.G., Boaden, R.J., Hunter, R.M., McKevitt, C., Paley, L. et al (2019) 'Impact and sustainability of centralising acute stroke services in English metropolitan areas: retrospective analysis of hospital episode statistics and stroke national audit data', *BMJ*, 364: 11.

Morris, Z.S., Wooding, S. and Grant, J. (2011) 'The answer is 17 years, what is the question: understanding time lags in translational research', *Journal of the Royal Society of Medicine*, 104(12): 510–20.

National Institute for Health and Care Excellence (NICE) (2016) *Psychosis and Schizophrenia in Children and Young People: Recognition and Management. Clinical Guideline (CG155)*. Available from: www.nice.org.uk/guidance/cg155 (accessed 4 February 2021).

National Institute for Health and Care Excellence (NICE) (2017) *Intrapartum Care for Healthy Women and Babies. Clinical Guideline (CG190)*. Available from: www.nice.org.uk/guidance/cg190 (accessed 4 February 2021).

National Institute for Health and Care Excellence (NICE) (2020) *Developing NICE Guidelines: The Manual. Process and Methods (PMG20)*. Available from: www.nice.org.uk/process/pmg20/chapter/glossary (accessed 4 February 2021).

National Institute for Health Research (NIHR) (2020) *Living with COVID-19, NIHR Evidence*. Available from: https://evidence.nihr.ac.uk/themedreview/living-with-covid19/ (accessed 30 October 2020).

National Institute for Health Research (NIHR) (2021) *Living with COVID-19, Second Review, NIHR Evidence*. Available from: https://evidence.nihr.ac.uk/themedreview/living-with-covid19-second-review/ (accessed 20 March 2021).

Newbould, J., Ball, S., Abel, G., Barclay, M., Brown, T., Corbett, J. et al (2019) 'A "telephone first" approach to demand management in English general practice: a multimethod evaluation', *Health Service & Delivery Research*, 7(17), https://doi.org/10.3310/hsdr07170

Newman, T.B. (2003) 'The power of stories over statistics', *BMJ*, 327(7429): 1424–7.

NHS (2019) *The NHS Long Term Plan*, https://www.longtermplan.nhs.uk/

Nicholson, J. and Ioannidis, J. (2012) 'Conform and be funded', *Nature*, 492(7427): 34–6.

Nicolini, D., Powell, J. and Korica, M. (2014) 'Keeping knowledgeable: how NHS Chief Executives mobilise knowledge and information in their daily work', *Health Services & Delivery Research*, 2(26), https://doi.org/10.3310/hsdr02260

Nixon, J., Smith, I.L., Brown, S., McGinnis, E., Vargas-Palacios, A., Nelson, E.A., Coleman, S., Collier, H., Fernandez, C., Gilberts, R. and Henderson, V. (2019) 'Pressure relieving support surfaces for pressure ulcer prevention (PRESSURE 2): clinical and health economic results of a randomised controlled trial', *EClinicalMedicine*, 14: 42–52.

Ocloo, J. and Matthews, J. (2016) 'From tokenism to empowerment: progressing patient and public involvement in healthcare improvement', *BMJ Quality & Safety*, 25(8): 626–32.

Oliver, K. and Boaz, A. (2019) 'Transforming evidence for policy and practice: creating space for new conversations', *Palgrave Communications*, 5: 60.

Oliver, K. and Cairney, P. (2019) 'The dos and don'ts of influencing policy: a systematic review of advice to academics', *Palgrave Communications*, 5: 21.

Oliver, K., Innvar, S., Lorenc, T., Woodman, J. and Thomas, J. (2014) 'A systematic review of barriers to and facilitators of the use of evidence by policymakers', *BMC Health Services Research*, 14(1): 1–12.

Oliver, K., Kothari, A. and Mays, N. (2019) 'The dark side of coproduction: do the costs outweigh the benefits for health research?', *Health Research Policy and Systems*, 17(1): 33.

Oran, D.P. and Topol, E.J. (2020) 'Prevalence of asymptomatic SARS-CoV-2 infection: a narrative review', *Annals of Internal Medicine*, 173: 362–7.

Oxman, A.D., Glenton, C., Flottorp, S., Lewin, S., Rosenbaum, S. and Fretheim, A. (2020) 'Development of a checklist for people communicating evidence-based information about the effects of healthcare interventions: a mixed methods study', *BMJ Open*, 10(7): e036348.

Pagel, C., Rogers, L., Brown, K., Ambler, G., Anderson, D., Barron, D. et al (2017) 'Improving risk adjustment in the PRAiS (Partial Risk Adjustment in Surgery) model for mortality after paediatric cardiac surgery and improving public understanding of its use in monitoring outcomes', *Health Services & Delivery Research*, 5(23), https://doi.org/10.3310/hsdr05230

Petchey, R., Hughes, J., Pinder, R., Needle, J., Partington, J. and Sims, D. (2013) *Allied Health Professionals and Management: An Ethnographic Study*, Southampton: National Institute for Health Research.

Phillips, D.P., Kanter, E.J., Bednarczyk, B. and Tastad, P.L. (1991) 'Importance of the lay press in the transmission of medical knowledge to the scientific community', *New England Journal of Medicine*, 325: 1180–3.

Pollitt, C. and Bouckaert, G. (2011) *Public Management Reform: A Comparative Analysis: NPM, Governance and the Neo-Weberian State* (3rd edn), Oxford: Oxford University Press.

Porter, M.E. (1985) *The Competitive Advantage: Creating and Sustaining Superior Performance*, New York: Free Press.

Powell, P. (2010) *The Interrogative Mood*, London: Profile Books.

Prichard, C. (2013) 'All the lonely papers, where do they all belong?', *Organization*, 20(1): 143–50.

Public Health England (2017) *Public Health Outcomes Framework: Health Equity Report Focus on Ethnicity*, London: Public Health England. Available from: https://assets.publishing. service.gov.uk/government/uploads/system/uploads/ attachment_data/file/733093/PHOF_Health_Equity_Report. pdf (accessed 1 February 2021).

Pyrko, I., Dörfler, V. and Eden, C. (2017) 'Thinking together: what makes communities of practice work?', *Human Relations*, 70(4): 389–409.

Radford, M. (2011) 'A manifesto for the simple scribe: my 25 commandments for journalists', *The Guardian* (online) 19 January. Available from: www.theguardian.com/science/ blog/2011/jan/19/manifesto-simple-scribe-commandments-journalists (accessed 24 October 2020).

Rangan, A., Handoll, H., Brealey, S., Jefferson, L., Keding, A., Martin, B.C. et al (2015) 'Surgical vs nonsurgical treatment of adults with displaced fractures of the proximal humerus: the PROFHER randomized clinical trial', *JAMA*, 313(10): 1037–47.

RECOVERY Collaborative Group (2021) 'Dexamethasone in hospitalized patients with Covid-19', *New England Journal of Medicine*, 384(8): 693–704.

Reed, M. (2018) *The Research Impact Handbook* (2nd edn), Aberdeenshire: Fast Track Impact.

REF2021 (2019) 'Assessment framework and guidance on submissions'. Available from: www.ref.ac.uk/publications/ guidance-on-submissions-201901/ (accessed 17 March 2021).

Renolen, Å., Høye, S., Hjälmhult, E., Danbolt, L.J. and Kirkevold, M. (2018) '"Keeping on track" – hospital nurses' struggles with maintaining workflow while seeking to integrate evidence-based practice into their daily work: a grounded theory study', *International Journal of Nursing Studies*, 77: 179–88.

Rickinson, M., Walsh, L., Cirkony, C., Salisbury, M. and Gleeson, J. (2020) *Quality Use of Research Evidence Framework*, Melbourne: Monash University. Available from: www.monash. edu/education/research/projects/qproject/publications/ quality-use-of-research-evidence-framework-qure-report (accessed 17 March 2021).

Roumbanis, L. (2019) 'Peer review or lottery? A critical analysis of two different forms of decision-making mechanisms for allocation of research grants', *Science, Technology, & Human Values*, 44(6): 994–1019.

Rudd, A.G., Bowen, A., Young, G. and James, M.A. (2017) 'National clinical guideline for stroke', *Clinical Medicine*, 17: 154–5.

Rushmer, R.K., Cheetham, M., Cox, L., Crosland, A., Gray, J., Hughes, L. et al (2015) 'Research utilisation and knowledge mobilisation in the commissioning and joint planning of public health interventions to reduce alcohol-related harms: a qualitative case design using a cocreation approach', *Health Services & Delivery Research*, 3(33), https://doi.org/10.3310/hsdr03330

Rutter, H., Savona, N., Glonti, K., Bibby, J., Cummins, S., Finegood, D.T. et al (2017) 'The need for a complex systems model of evidence for public health', *The Lancet*, 390(10112): 2602–04.

Rycroft-Malone, J., Burton, C., Wilkinson, J., Harvey, G., McCormack, B., Baker, R. et al (2015) 'Collective action for knowledge mobilisation: a realist evaluation of the Collaborations for Leadership in Applied Health Research and Care', *Health Services & Delivery Research*, 3(44), https://doi.org/10.3310/hsdr03440

Sacks, O. (2014) *The Man Who Mistook His Wife for a Hat*, London: Pan Macmillan.

Santesso, N., Rader, T., Nilsen, E.S., Glenton, C., Rosenbaum, S., Ciapponi, A. et al (2015) 'A summary to communicate evidence from systematic reviews to the public improved understanding and accessibility of information: a randomized controlled trial', *Journal of Clinical Epidemiology*, 68(2): 182–90.

Santesso, N., Morgano, G.P., Jack, S.M., Haynes, R.B., Hill, S., Treweek, S. and Schünemann, H.J. (2016) 'Dissemination of clinical practice guidelines: a content analysis of patient versions', *Medical Decision Making*, 36(6): 692–702.

Scales, K., Bailey, S., Middleton, J. and Schneider, J. (2017) 'Power, empowerment, and person-centred care: using ethnography to examine the everyday practice of unregistered dementia care staff', *Sociology of Health & Illness*, 39(2): 227–43.

Shaw, I. and Lunt, N. (2018) 'Forms of practitioner research', *British Journal of Social Work*, 48(1): 141–57.

Sheikh, K. (2019) 'How much nature is enough? 120 minutes a week, doctors say', *The New York Times*, 13 June. Available from: www.nytimes.com/2019/06/13/health/nature-outdoors-health.html (accessed 17 March 2021).

Shojania, K.G., Sampson, M., Ansari, M.T., Ji, J., Doucette, S. and Moher, D. (2007) 'How quickly do systematic reviews go out of date? A survival analysis', *Annals of Internal Medicine*, 147(4): 224–33.

Smith, K.E., Bandola-Gill, J., Meer, N., Stewart, E. and Watermeyer, R. (2020) *The Impact Agenda: Controversies, Consequences and Challenges*, Bristol: Policy Press.

Smith, R. (2006) 'Peer review: a flawed process at the heart of science and journals', *Journal of the Royal Society of Medicine*, 99(4): 178–82.

Soares-Weiser, K. (2011) 'Audit of the abstract, plain language summary and summary of findings tables in published Cochrane reviews', Cochrane Collaboration. Available from: www.dropbox.com/s/39mp8t1jc7817ik/Abstract%20audit%20report%20CEU%202012.pdf (accessed 17 March 2021).

Squires, J.E., Hutchinson, A.M., Boström, A.M., O'Rourke, H.M., Cobban, S.J. and Estabrooks, C.A. (2011) 'To what extent do nurses use research in clinical practice? A systematic review', *Implementation Science*, 6(1): 1–17.

Staley, K., Crowe, S., Crocker, J.C., Madden, M. and Greenhalgh, T. (2020) 'What happens after James Lind Alliance priority setting partnerships? A qualitative study of contexts, processes and impacts', *Research Involvement and Engagement*, 6(1): 41.

Storr, W. (2019) *The Science of Storytelling*, London: William Collins.

Straus, S., Tetroe, J. and Graham, I.D. (eds) (2013) *Knowledge Translation in Health Care: Moving from Evidence to Practice* (2nd edn), Chichester: John Wiley & Sons.

Sugimoto, C.R., Work, S., Larivière, V. and Haustein, S. (2017) 'Scholarly use of social media and altmetrics: a review of the literature', *Journal of the Association for Information Science and Technology*, 68(9): 2037–62.

Sumner, P., Vivian-Griffiths, S., Boivin, J., Williams, A., Venetis, C.A., Davies, A. et al (2014) 'The association between exaggeration in health related science news and academic press releases: retrospective observational study', *BMJ*, 349.

Sumner, P., Vivian-Griffiths, S., Boivin, J., Williams, A., Bott, L., Adams, R.C. et al (2016) 'Exaggerations and caveats in press releases and health-related science news', *PLoS One*, 11(12): e0168217.

Swan, J., Clarke, A., Nicolini, D., Powell, J., Scarbrough, H., Roginski, C. et al (2012) *Evidence in Management Decisions (EMD): Advancing Knowledge Utilization in Healthcare Management*, NIHR Service Delivery and Organisation Programme.

Sword, H. (2012) *Stylish Academic Writing*, Cambridge, Mass: Harvard University Press.

Synnot, A.J., Lowe, D., Merner, B. and Hill, S.J. (2018) 'The evolution of Cochrane evidence summaries in health communication and participation: seeking and responding to stakeholder feedback', *Evidence & Policy*, 14(2): 335–47.

Terkel, S. (1970) *Hard Times: An Oral History of the Great Depression*, New York: Pantheon Press.

Thompson, G.N., Estabrooks, C.A. and Degner, L.F. (2006) 'Clarifying the concepts in knowledge transfer: a literature review', *Journal of Advanced Nursing*, 53(6): 691–701.

Thomson, H. (2013) 'Improving utility of evidence synthesis for healthy public policy: the three Rs (relevance, rigor, and readability [and resources])', *American Journal of Public Health*, 103: e17–23.

Tierney, S., Wong, G., Roberts, N., Boylan, A.-M., Park, S., Abrams, R. et al (2020) 'Supporting social prescribing in primary care by linking people to local assets: a realist review', *BMC Medicine*, 18(1): 1–15.

Timmins, N., Rawlins, M. and Appleby, J. (2017) 'A terrible beauty: a short history of NICE the National Institute for Health and Care Excellence [version 1; not peer reviewed]', *F1000Research*, 6: 915.

Tricco, A.C., Cardoso, R., Thomas, S.M., Motiwala, S., Sullivan, S., Kealey, M.R. et al (2016) 'Barriers and facilitators to uptake of systematic reviews by policy makers and health care managers: a scoping review', *Implementation Science*, 11(1): 1–20.

Turnbull, J., McKenna, G., Prichard, J., Rogers, A., Crouch, R., Lennon, A. and Pope, C. (2019) 'Sense-making strategies and help-seeking behaviours associated with urgent care services: a mixed-methods study', *Health Services & Delivery Research*, 7(26), https://doi.org/10.3310/hsdr07260

Van de Ven, A.H. (2007) *Engaged Scholarship: A Guide for Organizational and Social Research*, Oxford: Oxford University Press.

Van de Ven, A.H. and Johnson, P.E. (2006) 'Knowledge for theory and practice', *Academy of Management Review*, 31(4): 802–21.

Van Noorden, R. (2014) 'Global scientific output doubles every nine years', *Nature news blog* (online) 7 May. Available from: http://blogs.nature.com/news/2014/05/global-scientific-output-doubles-every-nine-years.html (accessed 17 March 2021).

Vogel, J.P., Oxman, A.D., Glenton, C., Rosenbaum, S., Lewin, S., Gülmezoglu, A.M. and Souza, J.P. (2013) 'Policymakers and other stakeholders perceptions of key considerations for health system decisions and the presentation of evidence to inform those considerations: an international survey', *Health Research Policy and Systems*, 11(1): 1–9.

Vosoughi, S., Roy, D. and Aral, S. (2018) 'The spread of true and false news online', *Science*, 359(6380): 1146–51.

Wallace, J., Byrne, C. and Clarke, M. (2012) 'Making evidence more wanted: a systematic review of facilitators to enhance the uptake of evidence from systematic reviews and meta-analyses', *International Journal of Evidence Based Healthcare*, 10(4): 338–46.

Wallace, J., Byrne, C. and Clarke, M.J. (2014) 'Improving the uptake of systematic reviews: a systematic review of intervention effectiveness and relevance', *BMJ Open*, 4: e005834.

Waller, R. (2011) *Simplification: What Is Gained and What Is Lost*. Technical report. Available from: www.academia.edu/3385977/Simplification_what_is_gained_and_what_is_lost (accessed 17 March 2021).

Walshe, K. and Rundall, T.G. (2001) 'Evidence-based management: from theory to practice in health care', *The Milbank Quarterly*, 79(3): 429–57.

Ward, V., House, A. and Hamer, S. (2009) 'Knowledge brokering: the missing link in the evidence to action chain?' *Evidence & Policy*, 5(3): 267–79.

Weick, K. (1995) *Sensemaking in Organisations*, Thousand Oaks, California: Sage Publications.

Welsh, J., Lu, Y., Dhruva, S.S., Bikdeli, B., Desai, N.R., Benchetrit, L. et al (2018) 'Age of data at the time of publication of contemporary clinical trials', *JAMA Network Open*, 1(4): e181065.

Westen, D. (2008) *The Political Brain: The Role of Emotion in Deciding the Fate of the Nation*, New York: PublicAffairs Books.

White, M.P., Alcock, I., Grellier, J., Wheeler, B.W., Hartig, T., Warber, S.L. et al (2019) 'Spending at least 120 minutes a week in nature is associated with good health and wellbeing', *Scientific Reports*, 9(1): 1–11.

Whitty, C.J.M. (2015) 'What makes an academic paper useful for health policy?', *BMC Medicine*, 13: 301.

Wickremasinghe, D., Kuruvilla, S., Mays, N. and Avan, B.I. (2016) 'Taking knowledge users' knowledge needs into account in health: an evidence synthesis framework', *Health Policy and Planning*, 31(4): 527–37.

Widdowson, H.G. (1979) *Explorations in Applied Linguistics*, London: Oxford University Press.

Wieringa, S. and Greenhalgh, T. (2015) '10 years of mindlines: a systematic review and commentary', *Implementation Science*, 104(12): 501–9.

Williams, O. and Annandale, E. (2020) 'Obesity, stigma and reflexive embodiment: feeling the "weight" of expectation', *Health*, 24(4): 421–41.

Williams, O., Sarre, S., Papoulias, S.C., Knowles, S., Robert, G., Beresford, P. et al (2020) 'Lost in the shadows: reflections on the dark side of co-production', *Health Research Policy and Systems*, 18: 1–10.

Wilsdon, J.R. (2017) 'Responsible metrics', in T. Strike (ed) *Higher Education Strategy and Planning: A Professional Guide*, Abingdon: Routledge, pp 247–53.

Wilson, P. and Sheldon, T.A. (2019) 'Using evidence in health and healthcare', in A. Boaz, H. Davies, A. Fraser and S. Nutley (eds) *What Works Now? Evidence-Informed Policy and Practice*, Bristol: Policy Press, pp 67–88.

Wye, L., Brangan, E., Cameron, A., Gabbay, J., Klein, J. and Pope, C. (2015) 'Knowledge exchange in health-care commissioning: case studies of the use of commercial, not-for-profit and public sector agencies', Southampton: NIHR Journals Library, *Health Services Delivery & Research*, 3(19).

Index

References to figures and photographs appear in *italic* type.

A

academic writing 147–9
accessibility of language
  easy-read versions 33, 79–80, 83
  Flesch-Kincaid levels 141
  Plain English Campaign 139
  plain language summaries 78–9,
    82, 139–44, 154, 163
  readability 99, 141–2, 157–8
accessible formats 79–81, 95, 162–3
advocacy groups 23, 33, 75, 76–7,
  78, 79, 81, 91, 93
advocating for the evidence 92
altmetrics 19–20, 130
analytics 23, 131, 137, 165
anecdotes 72, 120, 121, 125,
  134, 153
  see also stories
animations 67–8
artwork 69
  see also images
asking the right research
    questions 21, 30, 32, 41–5,
    64–9, 85–9, 161
attention economy 13, 125
audience
  early engagement with 95–6, 107
  getting to know your 61–2, 161–2
  not all research is needed by wider
    audiences 37–8
  patients, the public and service
    users 63–83
  pen portraits 45, 61, 153
  policymakers and
    managers 84–103
  primacy of 7, 12
  reaching practitioners 41–62
  segmentation of 95–6, 130
  storytelling 135

  tailored outputs 33, 59, 113, 163
  target 7, 19, 21, 33, 40, 52–3,
    61–2, 79, 106
awareness weeks 133

B

behavioural drivers 65, 124
Bellos, David 155
Beresford, Peter 75–6
Best, Allen 16, 17, 43, 49
bias 36, 123, 141, 149
bibliometrics 15
big data 111
blogs 45, 68, 133–4, 136–7,
  156, 163
Boahen, Godfred 55–6
Boaz, Annette 9, 17, 73, 89
'bottom-up' research 75–6
Bowman, Deborah 156
Breckon, Jonathan 94
broadsheet journalism 77
Bromiley, Martin 121, 123
Brooks, Peter 119
bullet points 98
Buxton, Martin 104

C

Cairney, Paul 35, 37, 89–90, 94,
  96, 101, 107
Campbell, Joseph 120
cartoons 83
case studies 2, 18–19, 40, 61, 62,
  116, 164–5
catching the moment 106–8
chains of influence 62, 84, 90, 102
Chalabi, Mona 135
Chalmers, Iain 15–16, 29
champions 23, 57–8, 76–8, 94–5
Chapman, Sarah 156

charities 76, 78, 83, 94
Charon, Rita 117
Chew, Jack 58, 60–1
Chinn, Teresa 49, 58–9, 128, 165
Christensen, Clayton 28
citation metrics 15, 19, 127
Clark, David 85–6, 90
clinical advisors 57–8
clinical guidelines 13, 14, 19, 46–8
Cochrane Collaboration
  Dissemination checklist 154
  plain language summaries 139–40
  systematic reviews 14, 127
cognitive biases 36, 123
cognitive limitations 72
cognitive overload 48
collective negotiation of
  knowledge 51
comics 69, *70*
communication
  marketing and social
    persuasion 57, 96, 124, 130
  press releases 44, 151, 152
  Search Engine Optimisation
    (SEO) 130
  strategic communication 5,
    95–6, 130
  TED talks 119, 131, 137
communication teams 78, 83,
  130, 163
communities of practice 16–17, 35,
  44, 47, 50, 110
complexity and systems theory 17,
  44, 49, 85, 101–2
conferences 58, 61–2, 99, 103,
  131, 162
constructivist theories 50, 53
content analysis 79
context 22, 45–51, 69–72, 89–93,
  100, 112, 113
continuing professional
  development 48–9, 59
Conversation, The 125, 133, 163
co-production 68, 73, 141
co-researchers 53
cost savings 42, 48, 86, 92, 102
COVID-19 14, 30–1, 37, 42, 48,
  54, 108–11
credibility 55
crises, mobilising research
  during 108–11
crowdsourcing 111
Crowe, Sally 69, 71–2

cultural brokers 33
curiosity 119, 128, 164
Currie, Graham 34

D

data visualisations 131
  see also images
data-mining 111
Davies, Huw 5, 9, 35
decision-makers, reaching 84–103,
  112
deliberative processes 74–5, 105–6
democratising knowledge
  production 54, 165
dialogue versus broadcast 71–2,
  127–8
disruptive publishing models 37
diversity 31, 32–3, 75, 81
Dixon-Woods, Mary 28, 50–1
Dopson, Sue 28, 92
drawing 65, 135
  see also images
Dunleavy, Patrick 19, 133
dynamic reviews 110

E

early career researchers 48
easy-read versions 33, 79–80, 83
Economic and Social Research
  Council (ESRC) 127
editorial staff, working with 44
effective evidence use, models
  of 16–18
Elbow, Peter 147–8
embargoed versions 113, 116
embodied knowledge 93
emotions 90, 112, 154
ethics 54, 76
ethnicity 31, 33
ethnographic research 34, 91,
  93, 126
events 107
  see also conferences
evidence
  definition of term 7–8
  different kinds of 26–9
  'good enough' evidence 31
  quality of evidence,
    assessing 36–40
  what counts as 25–40, 92, 111
evidence centres 9
  see also What Works centres
'evidence eco-systems' 17–18

evidence literacy 96
evidence-based medicine 13–14
evidence-based policymaking 90–1
evidence-based practice 46
evidence-using behaviours 34
excluded groups 31, 32–3

F

fake news 165
Featherstone, Katie 132
feature articles 62
feedback loops 17, 59
films 132–3, 137
Flesch-Kincaid levels 141
framing 47–8, 56, 120
Fulop, Naomi 107–10
funders 9

G

Gabbay, John 34, 47
gamification 124
gatekeepers 36
Gawande, Atul 117
Glasziou, P. 15–16, 29
Gough, David 94
Graff, Gerald 154
Graham, Ian 17
grant awards 18, 29, 36
graphics 67
    see also images
graphs 135
Green, Lawrence 42, 49
Greenhalgh, Trish 19, 20, 31, 34, 47, 51, 57, 159
Grey, Christopher 164
grey literature 26, 35, 99, 101
Griffiths, Peter 87, 88
guidelines, embedding research in 46–8
    see also clinical guidelines
Gunning Fog index 141

H

Hanney, Stephen 111
hard to reach groups 31, 32–3
harm, potential for 76
Haux, Tina 19
headlines 125–6, 149–50, 163
healthcare managers, use of evidence by 91–3
Hey, Nancy 94–5
Holgate, Sir Stephen 122–3

Holmes, B. 16, 17, 43, 49, 130
hooks 8, 23, 62, 104, 125, 154
Hopkins, Claude C. 124
Huberman, Michael 50, 112
humanisation of research 72, 76, 120, 123, 145, 154, 164
humour 128, 155
Hutchinson, Janet 50, 112

I

icons 67
illustrations 61, 69
images 81, 121, 131, 134–7
    see also infographics
impact
    case studies 18
    impact literacy 6
    importance of thinking about 18–20
    reaching decision-makers 92–3, 96, 98
    short-term 89
    social media 49
    timing 111
    writing for 146–57
    see also metrics
implementation 18, 20, 55, 90, 98, 109, 111–12
implications versus recommendations 101
inclusion 31–2
    see also diversity
inequalities 31, 32–3
influence
    chains of 62, 84, 90, 102
    influencers 5, 21, 57–8, 62, 93, 102, 105, 127
    measurement of 57, 58
    ripple 88
    windows of influence 6, 96, 99, 105, 106, 113
infographics 83, 108, 135, *136*
information overload 14–15, 23, 37, 48, 89, 90, 161, 165
InSciOut 151–2
institutional biases 36
interim findings 113
intermediary bodies 9, 44, 55–6, 91, 93, 94
    see also thinktanks; What Works centres
Ioannides, John 36

J

James Lind Alliance (JLA) 42, 74–5
journalism 61, 77, 115, 122–4,
  149, 151–2
journalists
  engaging 77, 116
  interviews with 115–16, 122–3

K

keywords 130
Kingdon, J. 105, 106
knowledge
  breaking down silos 118, 133
  collective negotiation of
    knowledge 51
  communities of knowledge
    exchange 50
  democratising knowledge
    production 54, 165
  embodied knowledge 93
  gaps 21, 69, 100, 155, 159–60
  knowledge brokers 44, 57–8,
    92, 156
  mobilisation 19, 20, 34–6
  practice knowledge 46, 49–51
  tacit knowledge 50
  translation 35, 43, 79
kudos platform 130

L

language 138–58
  of academia 55, 76
  choice of words 154–5
  concrete nouns 126
  easy-read versions 33, 79–80, 83
  good writing 144–5
  natural language 147–8
  plain language summaries 78–9,
    82, 139–44, 154, 163
  of practice 47–8
  readability 99, 141–2, 157–8
  rhetoric 153
  style guides 144, 172
  support throughout study 33
  taking advice from advocacy
    groups 78
  telling stories 126
  translation for public use 79
Lave, Jean 50
Lavis, John 100
Layard, Richard 86, 90
layout 98, 102

le May, Andree 34, 47
learning disabilities 79–80, 83
Leary, Alison 116
Leder, Drew 68
Leith, S. 153
Lindstrom, Martin 124
linear ways of thinking about
  research dissemination 16–17,
  19, 47, 111–12
Lintern, Shaun 115
lived experience 22, 51, 64, 69, 77,
  110, 112, 141
living systematic reviews 111
lobbying 86, 105
local context 92, 98
Lomas, Jonathan 17
low quality research 15 16
'lurches of attention' 106–7

M

Maben, Jill 42
Maher, Chrissie 139
main message 61, 86, 120,
  126, 149
  see also headlines; summaries
managers, reaching 84–103
marginalised communities 31,
  65, 75
Marshall, Martin 161
Matthews, J. 75
Maxwell, Elaine 47–8
May, Carl 111
Maybin, Jo 93
McEnerney, Larry 124, 154
media 77, 106, 114–37
  see also journalism; social media
membership organisations 55
Mental Elf 133
metaphors 72, 159–60
methodological studies 38, 161
metrics
  altmetrics 19–20, 130
  bibliometrics 15
  citation metrics 15, 19, 127
  responsible 15
mindlines 34, 47
Mintrom, Michael 105
Mir, Ghazala 32–4
misinformation 165
Mitchell, Kirstin 143–4
mixed-method studies 65, 107
moral responsibility,
  researchers' 20, 165

multiple streams analysis 105, 106
My Life My Choice 79

N

narrative *see* stories
'narrowcasting' 77
National Institute for Health and
    Care Excellence (NICE) 7–8,
    14, 46, 87, 94
National Institute for Health
    Research (NIHR) 9, 14, 29,
    56, 73, *74, 78, 80*, 87, 91, 105,
    106, 107, 110, 142, 150
natural language 147–8
networks 22–3, 54–8, 91, 93, 94–5,
    110, 162
    see also partnerships;
    relational approaches
neuromarketing 124
new public management 46
Newman, Thomas 120–1, 122
newsletters 44
Nicolini, Davide 91, 93
Nightingale, Florence 1–2
normalisation process theory 111
Nursing Times 44–5, 48
Nutley, Sandra 17

O

'occasions of influence' 17
Ocloo, Josephine 75
Oliver, Kathryn 73, 89, 98, 101
online communities 44, 135
online events 103, 118, 137
online journal clubs 45, 48
Open Access 37
ORCID 131
organisational memory 93
'organised scepticism' 36
over-claiming 37
over-simplification, avoiding 72

P

Pagel, Christina *66*, 67
Parliamentary Office for Science
    and Technology 99–100
participatory research 33, 53,
    73
partnerships 22–3, 33, 38, 54–8,
    75–8, 93, 94–5
passive models of research
    adoption 16, 49, 50, 160
patient vignettes 132

patients
    advocacy groups 23, 33, 75,
        76–7, 78, 79, 81, 91, 93
    lived experience 22, 51, 64, 69,
        77, 110, 112, 141
    patient experiences 64, 73–4,
        77, 110
    patient groups 76–7, 81, 93, 110
    vignettes 77, 78
peer review 36
perspectives, differing 69–72
persuasion 124–7, 153–4
photographs 131
pictures/images 81, 121, 131, 134–7
Plain English Campaign 139
plain language summaries 78–9, 82,
    139–44, 154, 163
Plan S 37
playfulness 128, 137, 146, 153
podcasts 55, 60, 83
policy briefs 98–103
policy entrepreneurs 105
policy windows 6, 96, 99, 105,
    106, 113
policymakers, reaching 84–103
Porter, Michael 28
positive circles of connection 75–8
Powell, Padgett 153
power 33
practical wisdom 50–1
practice knowledge 46, 49–51
practice-based evidence 42
practice-facing journals 44–5
practitioner involvement in research
    and outputs 51–4
practitioners as researchers 49,
    52–3, 162
pragmatic trials 54
praxis 35, 50
preprints 37, 113
priority-setting 29, 42–3, 74–5,
    97, 106
professional associations 44
professional bodies/
    organisations 54–8, 93, 110
professional identities 53–4, 131
professional journals 44–5, 55, 62
professional wisdom 35, 50
projected outcomes 99
public engagement in research
    73–5, 77
public involvement in
    agenda-setting 74–5

publishing
   academic journals 23, 28, 36, 44,
      56, 93, 116, 127
   academic publishing 36–7
   information overload 14–15, 23,
      37, 48, 89, 90, 161, 165
   Open Access 37
'pull' for research 17, 55, 57, 75, 99
Pyrko, Igor 50

Q

qualitative research 65, 107
quality of evidence, assessing 36–40
quality of research 15
quotes/insights 52, 61, 65

R

Radford, Tim 120, 149
randomised controlled trials 12, 29
rapid evaluations 108–9
rapid reviews 30
rating systems 38
rationality 16, 46, 47
readability 99, 141–2, 157–8
reading your work out
   loud 149, 163
realist reviews 26–7
Reason, James 28
reciprocity 59, 60, 162
recommendations 101
RECOVERY trial 42
Reed, Mark 19
reflective learning 23, 45, 48–9,
   52, 113
regional collaborations 57
register 155
relational approaches 5, 16–17,
   43–4, 50, 76, 96, 109–10,
   128–30
relevance 29–34, 99
reliable information, finding 15–16
repeated sharing of research 59
research, definition of term 7–8
research dissemination centres 9
Research Excellence Framework
   (REF) 18
research institutes 36, 94
research literacy skills 49, 71–2
research waste 16, 29
researcher identity 20, 131, 162
researcher-practitioners 52–3, 162
responsibility 76
responsible research metrics 15

Rickinson, Mark 18
rigour 99
risk, concepts of 67
RN4Cast study 87
Rycroft-Malone, Jo 57

S

Sacks, Oliver 117
Sarson, Jade 69, 70
science, staying true to the 23, 79,
   81, 95, 122, 123, 139–40, 146,
   151–2, 163
science fairs 83, 131
scoping reviews 38, 96
Search Engine Optimisation
   (SEO) 130
Seely Brown, John 50
seminars 107
Sense about Science 67
sense-making processes 49,
   117, 118
sensitive areas 56
service user engagement in
   research 51, 73–5, 77–8,
   81, 110
   see also patients
Shaping Our Lives 76
Shepherd, Eileen 44–5, 48
Sheridan, Susan 121
Shojania, Kaveh 111
Simplification Centre 139
simplified versions versus simple
   accounts 141
situated learning 50
Smith, Judith 108–9
Smith, Katherine 19
social identity 50
social media
   altmetrics 19–20
   to amplify research 77
   attention economy 125
   broadcast versus dialogue 71–
      2, 127–8
   champions 58
   communicating research 127–31
   continuing professional
      development 49
   and COVID-19 37
   early career researchers 48
   fake news 165
   getting to know your
      audience 162
   headlines 151

journal reach 45
knowledge brokers 57
as means of finding out context
  for your research 113
publicity campaigns 108
to reach practitioners 58–62
reaching service users 68
and sensitive areas 56
stories 135, 137
using images on 135
and writing policy briefs 103
see also Twitter
social network analysis 57
social prescribing 26–7
Spiegelhalter, David 67
spin 37, 151
stakeholder involvement 21, 22, 29,
  39, 62, 109–10
Stapel, Diedrik 166
steering groups 55
stories 72, 79, 90, 92, 114–37, 145,
  153–4, 164
Storr, Will 119, 121
storylines 83
strategic choices, making 7, 95–6,
  159, 160
strategic communication 5, 95–
  6, 130
Straus, Sharon 20
study design 21, 100
style *see* language
style, writing 155–6, 157–8, 163
Sui Ting Kong 53
summaries 78–9, 95, 96, 98, 157–8
summary headlines 149–50
Sumner, Petroc 151
Sutton, Jon 120
Sword, Helen 120, 144–5,
  147, 156–7
systematic reviews 14, 29, 100, 111
systems model of thinking 17,
  44, 49

T

tacit guidelines 34
tacit knowledge 50
  see also practice knowledge
tagging 130
tailored outputs 33, 59, 113, 163
TED talks 119, 131, 137
Terkel, Studs 117
Tetroe, J. 17
thematic reviews 43

thinktanks 9, 44, 56, 93, 94
third person writing 76, 157
third sector organisations 77
time lags 13–16
timing 31, 99, 104–13
Tinkler, Jane 19, 133
titles 98, 100, 145, 146–7, 149, 158
topical issues 99, 105–6, 163
trade-offs 48, 133
traditional media 77, 106, 126–7
translation 155
translation of knowledge 35, 43, 79
translation of research into practice
  language 47–8
transparency 72, 146
trust 44, 93, 107
trusted intermediaries 55–6,
  92, 93
truth 165–6
Turnbull, Joanne 64–5
Twitter
  altmetrics 19
  analytics 131
  fake news 165
  influence 58–9
  promotion of research 68, 108,
    127–8, 137, 151
  relational approaches 44, 49,
    103, 137
  Tweetchats 44, 58, 59, 103, 128

V

validating findings 33
Van de Ven, Andrew 20, 35, 165
video chats 83
videos 132–3, 137
visual identity 131
visuals 134–7
  see also comics;
    images; infographics
voice 9, 58, 77, 133, 134, 146,
  155–7, 163–4

W

Waller, Rob 139, 140–1
Walshe, K. 28
webinars 103, 131
websites 68, 131
Webster, Ben 122–3
Weick, Karl 117
@WeNurses 58–9, 128
Westen, Drew 91
What Works centres 46, 94–6, *97*

white space 98, 102
Whitty, Chris 101
Widdowson, Henry 140–1
wider audiences, not all research
     suitable for 37–8
Wieringa, Sietse 34, 51, 159

Williams, Oli 68, 69, 73
windows of influence 6, 96, 99,
     105, 106, 113
wisdom of practice 46, 49–51
Witchalls, Clint 125–6, 134
Wye, Lesley 92